The
Madness
of
Things
Peruvian

013622675

University of Liverpool

Withdrawn from stock

Alvaro Vargas Llosa

The Madness of Things Peruvian

Democracy Under Siege

Transaction Publishers
New Brunswick (U.S.A.) and London (U.K.)

Copyright © 1994 by Transaction Publishers, New Brunswick, New Jersey 08903.

All rights reserved under International and Pan-American Copyright Conventions. No part of this book may be reproduced or transmitted in any form or by any means, electronic or mechanical, including photocopy, recording, or any information storage and retrieval system, without prior permission in writing from the publisher. All inquiries should be addressed to Transaction Publishers, Rutgers—The State University, New Brunswick, New Jersey 08903.

Library of Congress Catalog Number: 93-12632
ISBN: 1-56000-114-3
Printed in the United States of America

Library of Congress Cataloging-in-Publication Data
Vargas Llosa, Alvaro
  The madness of things Peruvian : democracy under siege / Alvaro Vargas Llosa
    p.   cm.
  Includes bibliographical references (p.   ) and index.
  ISBN 1-56000-114-3
  1. Peru—Politics and government—1980-   2. Fujimori, Alberto. 3. Peru—Moral conditions.   4. Democracy—Peru.   I. Title.
F3448.2.V365   1993
985.06'33—dc20
                                                           93-12632
                                                              CIP

To Linda and Carlos Alberto Montaner

Esteban: *El Traje se te ha subido a la cabeza. Cuidado con la borrachera del Traje: es la peor de todas.*

—Alejo Carpentier, *El siglo de las luces*

Los Podridos han prostituido y prostituyen palabras, conceptos, hechos e instituciones al servicio de sus medros, de sus granjerías, de sus instintos y de sus apasionamientos. Los Congelados se han encerrado dentro de ellos mismos, no miran sino a quienes son sus iguales y a quienes son sus dependientes, considerando que nada más existe. Los Incendiados se queman sin iluminar, se agitan sin construir. Los Podridos han hecho y hacen todo lo posible para que el país sea una charca; los Congelados lo ven como un páramo; y los Incendiados quisieran prender explosivos y verter veneos para que surja una gigantesca fogata.

—Jorge Basadre,
Perú: problema y posibilidad.

No te abraces a las estatuas heladas.

—Epicteto

Contents

1

The Rotting and the Death of Democracy

It was 29 August 1975. There was nothing apparent to change the routine on that winter day at the Franco-Peruano School that I shared with a couple of hundred middle-class Peruvian kids and where I was doing my primary studies. The bell had rung at a quarter to four in the afternoon, after the customary two hours of class following the lunch break, where we had those heated football games that seemed to be the real purpose of the school. As we ran for the bus, there was a strange word buzzing in the air. It passed through the yard first like a rumor, then as an emergency, then as an alarm: "Coup! Coup! Coup!" I imagined some natural disaster. I had experienced an earthquake the previous year, when I had just turned eight. It had caught me on the ninth floor of a long building in Lima that looked out onto the sea hovering over a sheer cliff and giving the impression, during the minute and a half of tremors, that it was about to cave in. That afternoon, as a new word, *Golpe!* made its way into my vocabulary and my consciousness, I had for the first time the sensation of belonging to a community that was broader than the family or the school. I was convinced that the earth was being assaulted by a new fury of the gods. "What's the matter? What's the matter?" I kept asking insistently. "Run to the buses!" came the order of the supervisors. "There's been a military coup against President Velasco. We have to get home quick. There are orders not to go out."

I listened in shock. The word *golpe* (blow, coup) had for me only the literal and physical connotations. Had someone struck the president? Why so much fuss? Had someone punched Velasco in the nose? A general stampede prevented me from hearing any details of the event. I ran to the bus with my schoolmates. Once inside, things became a bit more clear. A man by the name of Francisco Morales Bermúdez, an army general,

1

had replaced President Velasco (also a general) as chief of state. Several shots had been fired. I recall my feelings of horror, intrigue, incredulity, and fear on hearing this. Not in my wildest dreams had I thought that what I was hearing could be possible. It was as though a child of my age, nine years, had had his father removed from the house or one of my classmates had taken control from the teacher. It was a shock as great as finding out where babies come from.

The world changed for me that day. Authority, government, law, good and evil lost their atemporal and distant qualities, their sacred sense, their abstract nature. They became something material, with faces and names, subject to change, vulnerable, and unforeseen; in a word: violent. Coup! Coup! Coup!

In the early hours of the morning on 6 April 1992, the telephone rang in my room in a Seville hotel in Spain. I had to take an early plane that morning, and, as I lazed between the sheets, I damned the wake-up call. But it wasn't a wake-up call; it was my father calling from Berlin. He had been in Seville the night before, so it wasn't a normal call.

"There's been a coup in Peru. They've banned the Congress. There are tanks around the Parliament building. Some deputies are under arrest. The Constitution is suspended. They've canceled the powers of the Supreme Court and the controller general. Fujimori has come out on television assuming responsibility for the coup."

I was almost as shocked as on that winter afternoon of the twenty-ninth of August in 1975. There was the same sensation of lack of government, chaos, impotence. The same incredulity. The same abyss opened before my very eyes. But this time it wasn't only my notions of authority, power, and order falling over the edge. It was also the country that, in the three previous years during my father's hard-fought presidential campaign, I had discovered in its rough, contradictory, and abandoned existence, with the marked wrinkles and scars of its social face. It was a country with which we had lived an intense love story, followed by a violent break, and with which, to a certain extent, we had learned to suffer.

So despite the years that had passed between that schoolboy's shocking confrontation with political power in Peru and the events of 1992 in a country whose deep wounds he had come to in time, the news was still startling. It didn't matter if it was foreseeable in the context of our agonizing democracy and the violent dispute between our society and its institutions: it was, like the first time, something of a revelation.

As I flew to Madrid I tried to imagine the faces of those Peruvians watching the president on TV telling them that night (5 April) that the Constitution he had promised to respect and make respected was now in the garbage can; that judicial power, which not even General Velasco Alvarado had touched in his 1968 coup, no longer existed; and that Parliament, whose members had gotten there thanks to the same voters who had decided on 10 April 1990 that Señor Fujimori would be the rival of Mario Vargas Llosa in the second round of elections, was now a part of history.

I tried to imagine the stunned parliamentarians looking out of their windows and seeing soldiers pointing automatic weapons at them and ordering them to stay inside. I thought of journalists being dragged in the dark of night into police vans with no license plates filled with uniformed traitors. I could feel the disgust of reporters writing or reading news under the cold gaze of armed censors. And I could sense the repugnant atmosphere of press rooms, where felony and cowardice would be taking on, as usual, an aspect of normality—an appearance indicating that nothing was happening—while the professional voices and typewriters of dozens of people named Judas, with a casual humor (a distinctive sign of mediocrity in such moments) were accommodating themselves to the new power play, stabbing democracy in the back in the name of . . . democracy. Meanwhile, several of their colleagues were behind bars.

Like thousands of Peruvians, my head was filled with questions. Was this a coup by the military using Fujimori temporarily as a civilian puppet, or was it the work of the president himself? Was it a blow by the drug dealers and their military pawns who had taken Fujimori under control and forced him to obey? What would the reaction of the political parties be? Would the military kill former President Alan García, whose growing opposition to the executive had come to complicate things for a government that owed him considerably for its existence?

At eleven o'clock Sunday night, after the usual TV news programs—when most of the politicians, journalists, bureaucrats, and foreign diplomats were at home—Señor Fujimori (president of Peru since 28 July 1990) asked the main television channel to run a speech to the nation taped earlier by the producer Alfonso Baella, whose father was a political editor with *El Comercio*, the oldest and most respected newspaper in the country. It was Fujimori's first public appearance since March, when his wife, Susana, brought charges against the president's brother, his brother's wife, and his sister, regarding the illicit appropriation of clothing donations from Japan for poor people in Peru and the sale of this donated material for profit.

While the speech was being transmitted on television, troops had been deployed quickly in order to neutralize any possible sources of resistance and to control strategic (or symbolic) points: Congress, the Palace of Justice, the telephone company, the homes of legislators (especially those of the presidents of the two bodies—Senator Felipe Osterling and Deputy Roberto Ramírez Del Villar, both from the center-right Popular Christian party), the home of former President Fernando Belaunde Terry, the homes of other important congressmen, the central headquarters of parties—especially that of Alianza Popular Revolucionaria Antiimperialista (APRA), the country's most organized political machine, which was suspected of hiding a large number of arms and of being capable of offering the greatest resistance should the opposition take to the streets.

One place that couldn't be left out was the home of Alan García, the socialist APRA leader and former president. A large detachment was sent to Chacarilla, an upper-class residential district in metropolitan Lima, with orders to take him into custody. When the men arrived they found his daughters and the maids. His mother and his lawyer and party comrade, Deputy Jorge del Castillo, arrived a while later. Both were prevented from entering the house. The men in uniform searched every corner of the house, shot into the air, cordoned off the area, and decreed the immediate house arrest of García's daughters. Del Castillo was taken off to an army barracks. Alan García had barely managed to escape and hide in a neighboring house, after being alerted by Del Castillo. Agustín Mantilla, García's former interior minister, whom García had telephoned minutes before his escape to warn him of what was coming, was not able to get away. When he was leaving his house, where he had been celebrating the birthday of a fellow APRA leader, he was arrested by 200 commandos. They were convinced that this arrest was key. Mantilla's murky participation as the brains behind the security apparatus of García's party, his reputation as a thug while he was interior minister, and his ties to the import of North Korean arms, which ended up not only with the army but in the hands of his party, made him an important prisoner in the early hours of the coup, especially if the reason behind his capture was to discourage any attempts at resistance. Nonetheless, there was time for APRA leaders to warn García, and for him to flee. Agustín Mantilla was in prison for a year and three months since the day of his arrest without a trial. Another key APRA figure arrested that night was Alberto Kitasono, the organization secretary. His low profile and bent for back-room politics had earned him a rather shady reputation. His arrest stopped him from organizing a party mobilization against the coup. Several police officers suspected of sympathizing with APRA were also put behind bars.

The mass media were neutralized. Army censors were sent to all press rooms. All but two radio stations and two magazines gave in. One of the rebellious stations was closed down immediately; and the other survived until the next morning, when the directors were arrested. The magazines were not able to print for a few days.

Independent journalist Gustavo Gorriti, who was known for his investigative work on *Sendero Luminoso*'s (Shining Path) terrorist insurrection, was one of several journalists taken into custody. At three in the morning, fifteen soldiers with submachine guns burst into his home claiming to be from state security. They took him away in a van with no license plate to the "Pentagonito" ("little Pentagon"), the army headquarters. He was held there all night and turned over to the police the following day. His computer and personal records, the fruit of several years of work, were confiscated.

Meanwhile, on another side of town, trade union headquarters—the CGTP, the CTP, the CNT, and the CTRP—were stormed by soldiers, and their leaders were placed under armed guard. Soldiers sacked the archives of judges and prosecutors at the Palace of Justice and took them away in army trucks, which sped away in the night. This purging of judicial archives continued for a week. The next day, seventeen judges and thirteen magistrates of the Supreme Court were removed by presidential decree. This was justified by "The Basic Law of the National Reconstruction Government," a clear repetition of the legal formula used in 1968 by General Velasco Alvarado to replace the democratic president, Fernando Belaunde, and it was backed by tanks. Habeas corpus was suspended. Prime Minister Alfonso de los Heros resigned out of loyalty to the democratic system and was replaced with surprising swiftness by

Oscar de la Puente. The ambassador in Washington also resigned on matters of principle. The foreign minister gave up his post later because of differences with the economy minister. These were the only resignations of government members emerging from the events in question. The rest of the government, the majority of which was entirely taken by surprise, was happy to continue to serve in the new situation.

The following day a communiqué from the joint command of the armed forces and the director general of the police assumed responsibility for what had happened the night before and expressed loyalty to the president of the republic. But at the same time, all political parties without exception (including the president's own Cambio 90) denounced the coup d'état. Shortly after, Law 255444 decreed penal sanctions for parliamentarians or judges remaining active in office. The parliamentarians who were not in jail and who were prohibited by decree from leaving the country feared that violence on the part of the soldiers would prevent them from gathering in Congress, so they met at the headquarters of the College of Barristers and declared that as of 9 April the presidency was vacant. They were using article 206 of the Constitution, which expressly authorized Parliament to take such action in extreme cases. The two vice presidents contacted the opposition, joining ranks with the resistance. The first, Máximo San Román, was traveling, so it was the second vice president who had to assume the presidency in place of Fujimori, which the Congress authorized. Pursued by authorities, the second vice president, Carlos García, was forced to take refuge in the embassy of Argentina. Menem, the president of that country, who had called his ambassador home for consultations, ordered that he be received. The government of Brazil had called its ambassador home as well.

In the meantime, the first vice president, Máximo San Román, was organizing his return. In fighting spirit, he said his challenge was from *cholo* to *chino*[1]. In a conversation I had with him by telephone in Miami, he added that he had fixed his return after "a very difficult and dangerous decision." He planned to head a mobilization, which actually began on 18 April amid the acclaim of parliamentarians who went out to welcome him at Jorge Chávez Airport. No sooner had he gone through immigration control than his enthusiasm suffered the tough blows of reality: the police confiscated his passport.

So, in what constituted an appropriately grotesque symbol of political events in the country, for several days Peru had three presidents: Fujimori ruling from the government palace and the "Pentagonito" military headquarters; Carlos García y García authorized by the Congress of the republic until the return of San Román; and in theory San Román from abroad as the legal holder of constitutional powers designated by Parliament. This was a unique case in the history of Peru. The political schizophrenia was experienced not only at home but also abroad—although less markedly: two instead of three governments were visible, since foreign public opinion was unable to differentiate between the two vice presidents. On 12 April the Organization of American States (OAS) met in Washington in an urgent session to debate the situation in Peru. Attending were both the foreign minister of the spurious government and San Román as the special envoy of the constitutional government, which he now headed. The OAS apparently adapted reasonably to this bicephalous diplomacy on that occasion and was willing to listen to both sides.

Despite international condemnation of the coup, the initial unification of the political parties behind this vice president-turned-president and the desperate attempt to stop democracy from evaporating, the mirage didn't last long. There was, in fact, one single government, and it continued governing. The president of the National Court of Elections was removed on 13 April by the "National Reconstruction Government." At the same time, the de facto ruler announced, with almost daily changes in his political calendar, the calling of plebescites to consult the people on what was happening in the country. There was a sense of *fait accompli*; and the resistance became, despite international backing, imbued with the worst possible attitude: demoralization.

The man who had come to power as a result of his promise to change Peru's political tradition—which meant tricks, conspiracy, force, and authoritarianism—had learned what the score was after less than two years in office. Playing Peruvian politics by its own rules, he had won. Backed by a methodology that has endless precedents in Peru, he had added to the country's historical record a new form of doing the same thing. With his coming to power in 1990, Peru had witnessed once again, after eight decades, a second change in power from one untouchable government to another. But he chose to return to tradition when that tradition seemed to be breaking up and its faithful agents—the military, businessmen, and politicians—seemed to have lost their antidemocratic instincts. He became intimidated by the suspicion that the old ways had been discredited and that this half-dead country had managed in spite of it all to preserve democracy. Suddenly a man (the most political of all), coming out of nowhere, brought back to life old customs in this country of old customs, which seemed to have opted for a break with the past. The operation was perfect. No Peruvian from the traditional political class—civilian or military—would have been able to unearth this old practice in today's Peru. This could only be the role of someone coming from nowhere to express the national vengeance against the ghosts that varied according to the Peruvian in question and that were understandably incarnated in Peru's political class. It wasn't a case of changing the tradition. It was a case of breaking the traditional monopoly and placing it in the hands of someone with no past, in a form of revenge. Alberto Fujimori was sharp enough to intuit that these feelings were in the air, and he took advantage of them, unleashing this chain of events to which I've just referred. He provided the country with a sense of déjà vu.

Who is he? Where did he come from? How, when, and why did this man with no Peruvian past become an heir of the old line of Peruvian dictators? His emergence is forever linked to the process of degeneration and the defeat of Peruvian democracy between 1980 and 1992. This story represents the victory of a minority of enemies of democracy against a majority, which in 1980 had wildly celebrated that democratic dawn. We see mixed the weaknesses and failures of a system that its representatives couldn't exploit and the simultaneous action -in the beginning not even deliberate- of people and groups who took advantage of fissures in the Peruvian society and the fragile nature of its institutions in order to bring democracy down from within. This facilitated the return to total power of military men who, late in 1978, when the election to the Constituent Assembly had taken place and inaugurated the transition to democracy, had fled in retreat and left civilians, during the 1980s, at the helm of the nation. The militarization of Peruvian life during the twelve-year democratic interval and the coming to power of Alberto Fujimori ended by walling off democracy.

On 29 March 1990, just two weeks before the first round of the presidential elections that were to bring Fujimori to power, I was urgently called to the headquarters where we directed the campaign of my father, who was one of the competing candidates and had seemed, in the previous weeks, to be heading for a landslide. We learned for the first time, amid a mess of papers from our U.S. political consultants (the Sawyer and Miller agency), that Alberto Fujimori was beginning to lose his status as a "small candidate" and had overtaken the APRA candidate and the left candidates, with a 20 percent backing, placing him in a strong second place. In a matter of hours, just a few days from election day, this agricultural engineer, the son of Japanese immigrants, former dean of the Agrarian University, and former host of an agriculture program at 5 A.M. on local television, had moved up fifteen points in the polls. There was no precedent for this phenomenon. We were speaking of an unknown competitor who was in last place only days before, along with picturesque presidential aspirants like the representative of the Israelis of the New Universal Pact, a would-be biblical patriarch, who proposed that Peru return to the times of the Old Testament. Twelve days before the voting, to everyone's surprise, Fujimori was suddenly in second place and moving ahead. *El chino*, as he is called in Peru, became a household name.

The Peruvian electoral campaign had uncovered a hatred of everything having to do with traditional politics. It was a feeling that hit all official institutions—the parties, the Church, the armed forces, the government, justice. But no sector was more despised than politicians, both within and outside the government, who had contributed, since the beginning of the democratic period in 1980, to the creation of a schism within a country where the majority of citizens, standing apart from their institutions, had created lives completely outside the law in response to a state which had been losing their trust since the founding of the republic. The phenomenon of this cultural rejection of the Peruvian state came far earlier than the appearance of democracy. But it was democracy, functioning after 1980, that made the situation obvious. The fact that the institutional fracture came about during democracy was not, of course, mere historical chance. That democracy, pressured by its tragic heritage, couldn't—it didn't know how to and it didn't want to—solve the problem in time. So the country took its final civilian and democratic chance in the 1990 elections. It was obvious that if this chance were lost, the conditions for a dictatorship were in place.

It was in this context that the Peruvian political campaign took place. Led by my father, a group of us, all independent Peruvians and mostly liberals in the classical sense of the term[2]—took an active part. We were linked in an alliance with two of the country's traditional parties, which had governed during the first period of democracy, from 1980 to 1985, along with a less important party, all made up of individuals at that point out of favor with politics. The extremily long campaign we conducted, the efficient, violent, and dishonest strategy of our adversaries to discredit us with the electorate, and the feeling that this alliance had from the first obscured the independent freshness of the newcomers forced us, on the threshhold of power, into everyday politics. All these factors contributed to the erosion of our efforts to convince Peru that it was time for an extensive liberal revolution, one that would seek to re-establish social harmony, transform our state, and recover general confidence in the nation. The beneficiaries of this change in image were not our adversaries. President Alan García, who had governed since 1985 as the head of Peru's most traditional party, the APRA, and who claimed to have unleashed a leftist, democratic, popular, nationalist, and anti-imperialist revolution had dragged the country to ruin and could do nothing for his party in these elections. His service record was singular. In five years the accumulated inflation was at 2 million percent. He had done away with half a million jobs. Workers had seen their salaries falling by 50 percent of their value, and those of public employees by one-third. Furthermore, the close ties between many of the Peruvian socialists and communists and García's regime, as well as the ideological kinship between APRA and the left (emerging during the failed attempt to confiscate Peru's financial system and put it in the hands of the government in 1987) eliminated the two candidates from the left as serious options.

So while our star fell on the eve of these elections, that of Alberto Fujimori burned brighter. No one knew anything about him. The only government plan he offered was "honesty, technology, and work." We found out later that APRA had tried to convince the independent candidate for mayor in Lima to put him on his list. This gave us the vague idea that Fujimori could be an APRA instrument who, with phrases more or less coinciding with the main ideas of our campaign (change, modernity, liberalism), would rob us of sufficient votes to prevent us from winning in the first round of elections. Without that first-round victory it would be very difficult to carry out the program of serious reforms we were proposing. As it happened, we were forced into the second round. During the run-off election campaign, the government as well as the left joined the campaign to cut us off; and the state put its powerful resources at the disposal of Fujimori.

Today it is clear that the army intelligence service played a key role. It provided detailed information on our activities, mounted a logistics apparatus for Fujimori's movements and security, and made up for the candidate's lack of a party political structure. This was the real force behind Fujimori's second-round campaign, not Cambio 90, scarcely more than a handful of the candidate's friends whom he had convinced to join the electoral lists with him for the Senate. His original intention was to stand for the Senate, not for the presidency, but since it was possible to be a candidate for both at the same time, he did so. He was thinking of the curiosity that might surround him as a minor presidential candidate, and of the fruits to be gathered from it toward his senatorial candidacy. President Alan García placed the army intelligence service specifically at his disposition. Ties between the two were evident. The day after the first round of elections, García telephoned former president Fernando Belaunde in Moscow, at that time a political associate of ours, to ask him to convince my father not to drop out of the second round. He was intending to back out due to the lack of trust shown by the electorate in a government program that would require a broad majority, from the executive on down, to deal with created interests that would try to block reforms. But no one suspected the military ties.

It is only now that we know about these sophisticated and intricate ties that soon after would have decisive consequences regarding the events of 5 April 1992, and for the course of Peruvian democracy. At that point, the backing of the Peruvian state for Alberto Fujimori was somewhat ironic. After all, it was apparently a marriage between what Peruvians despised, government and politics, and a product of that hate, the people's would-be agent of change. There was also something magical in this candidacy. The backing of the state didn't totally explain this phenomenon of the masses, quiet and interiorized, which, in contrast with all other popular causes in Peru, was expressed in a contained and almost shameful manner. It grew around us mysteriously. The improvisation, emptiness, and inexperience of the dark- horse candidate seemed to go against the effectiveness with which his campaign was mounted. He rummaged through the garbage pail of Peruvian populism to grab at whatever might rouse the country against any proposal for a liberal and rational change aimed squarely against sentimentality and demagogy. He was out to arouse the country with impossible and contradictory options: to beat inflation without shock therapy; to create a million and a half jobs without heavy reforms; to meet the financial deficit without touching public enterprises, which meant a $ 2.5 billion loss every year; to finish off the cocaine plantations with two guards per hectare; to regulate the ministries by means of tests; and to get $3 billion from Japan. Today we know that the element behind this well-organized populist campaign, which in a perfectly political way cried out against professional politics, was not chance or magic, but something more pedestrian: the National Intelligence Service (SIN).

The decisive role in the organization of this apparatus, which would become the agent of the downfall of the political system later on, was played by one Vladimiro Montesinos Torres, a middle-aged character who got to power through the back door of politics and whose name, lingering on everyone's tongue, few dared publish during the first years of Fujimori's administration. He was born in Arequipa and graduated without distinction from the Chorillos Military School in Lima in 1966 as a second lieutenant in the artillery. After his graduation as an officer, he took up law. His participation in the military government of Velasco Avarado, after the latter had brought down a democratically elected Fernando Belaunde in 1968, was due in large part to the connections of his uncle, Alfonso Montesinos, who had been a socialist legislator. His leftist ideas gave him a certain influence in the military government, which at the time wanted to carry out a socialist revolution in Peru. Having achieved the rank of artillery captain, he became the assistant to the army general commander Mercado Jarrín, one of the staunchest figures in the dictatorship. He managed to survive the coup d'état of Morales Bermúdez in 1975 and began to work his way into the intelligence service, thanks to the influence he had gained as secretary of the advisory committee of prime minister, General Arbulú Galiani. He was named adviser to the intelligence service led by General Schroth. And for the first time in his career, there was an accusation against him that very year: a group of middle-level army officers arrested for conspiring against President Morales Bermúdez in order to restore Velasco said he was working for the CIA.

These charges became important in 1976. Montesinos was accused by the then Major Fernández Salvatecci of selling classified information from the SIN via the U.S. military attaché. According to the charges, the information sold included: a complete report on Soviet arms for the Peruvian army, the acquisition of war materials from the USSR, the weekly agenda of the president, and details of the August 1975 coup, which Morales Bermúdez pulled off against Velasco.

The trial of Montesinos, during which he was held in a military barracks, ended with his separation from the army. He left with his established contacts and immediately started practicing law, establishing a network of complicity within the judiciary and the prosecuting systems. He defended, during the 1980s, a large number of police who had been fired, and managed to get them reinstated despite the opposition of the democratic government of Alan García. During this stage he drew closer to certain drug dealers: Carlos Lamberg, doing a jail sentence, and his lawyer, Mario Salomón Zorrilla, who in 1990 was a candidate for Congress representing Fujimori's party, Cambio 90. At the end of the 1980s the most important case in Peruvian drug dealing took place with the arrest of Reinaldo Rodríguez López, "the Godfather," along with certain police officers. Montesinos was the star defense attorney of the majority of the accused. He established a close relationship with the office of the national prosecutor. He offered information on agencies involved in the control of drugs in return for preferential treatment for his clients accused of drug dealing. Montesinos visited the attorney general, and his access to the public ministry was unlimited.

This is the man who, in the electoral campaign of 1990, went along with candidate Alberto Fujimori. The story shows very well how a cancer was eating away at the cells of Peruvian democracy. Montesinos, like many sons of the military dictatorships of Velasco Alvarado and Morales Bermúdez, easily made use of contacts, practices, influences, and sources of information obtained during the military period to take advantage (once democracy was restored) of the porosity of the system and the failure of the legitimate governments of Belaunde and García to purge Peruvian institutions of vices inherited from the past, and actively conspired against the consolidation of decent civilian and legal institutions. They were hiding in ambush, awaiting the moment to give the coup de grâce to a democracy that in 1990, when Fujimori took power, was in a poor position to defend itself.

There was another individual moving along the same lines who placed Alberto Fujimori in contact with Montesinos: Francisco Loayza. He was a social researcher for an institute belonging to one of the key generals in the military process of the 1970s, Leonidas Rodríguez Figueroa. Fujimori needed a lawyer because the campaign had brought about a considerable number of charges of tax fraud, undervaluation of dozens of properties bought and sold by the Fujimoris, and poor administration of funds when he was dean of the University of Agronomy. He had also come into possession of a private estate as a "beneficiary of the 1969 agrarian reform," which was aimed at putting land into the hands of the peasants. Harassed by the charges, which the prosecutors were forced to deal with, Fujimori asked for a lawyer who had key contacts. He was given Vladimiro Montesinos. Within days, the prosecutors began to put off the charges, and the judges, waiting for proceedings that never came, opened no criminal action. Montesinos, whom, from that point, Fujimori owed important favors, became the orchestrator of his political apparatus and the connection between him and the intelligence service. The link, at the time, was out of public view.

From the time he came to power Fujimori's skill in the military sphere seemed surprising, even though he was, of course, by constitutional mandate, commander in chief of the armed forces. After all, he had only recently come to politics and, despite handling a rhetorical populism very well, he had the apparent image of someone apart from the intricate and petty life of the Peruvian state, with its political and economic interests, its heirarchies, and its rarefied conspiratorial atmosphere. From the first moment, with an enviable self-confidence, he brought about a general shuffling in the armed forces that would later prove crucial when he launched his assault on the democratic system. On 28 July, the very day he assumed power, two of the three commander generals of the armed forces (one headed the navy, the other the air force) were removed from their posts for no explicit reason. The one from the air force had been discredited after the recording of a telephone conversation with a mistress. His firing was understandable. But the other, the one from the navy, had been a widely respected man. Regarding replacements, normal promotion lists were respected in neither case. This meant that others were displaced. In the following twenty-four hours there was a general house cleaning of top police officials. Only a single general survived. The rest, including some 200 officers, were retired. The hand of Montesinos is obvious in the 1991 and 1992 promotions: he gave strong preference to a number of supporters. From the start of his administration the president acted purely on recommendations from his adviser, since both as a newcomer to Peru's political establishment and as a brand-new head of state he was not very familiar with the intricacies of military life.

In the second quarter of 1991 the government issued legislative decrees stipulating that the commander generals of the three branches of the armed forces and the police would not go into retirement at the end of service, but would stay on for three more years, in contradiction to tradition and a previous law. Those who were promoted in 1991 and 1992 would remain in their positions, thus facilitating the civilian-military plot that had been hatched behind the scenes. When Congress was about to review the presidential decree in accordance with the Constitution, the coup d'état abruptly consolidated the decision.

At the beginning of 1992 Nicola de Bari Hermoza became head of the army. On the whole, Montesinos promoted his followers from the artillery. His influence in the Intelligence Service was decisive. Chief Julio Salazar, an old teacher of his at the military academy, received orders from him, since he acted as the president's security adviser. Salazar was named to the post of brigadier general. On two occasions Congress had rejected his appointment as major general, which in any government would have meant his automatical removal from the head of the Intelligence Service. Immediately after the 5 April coup he was promoted by decree.

This was the delicate military strategy mapped out by the Alberto Fujimori government in 1990, 1991, and the beginning of 1992. Since 1980, when democracy returned after twelve years of military dictatorship, relations between the military and civilian society had posed a great challenge. They were difficult relations because of the long history of military involvement in institutional life. From the beginning, civilian institutions were greatly influenced by the ethos of Peru's military tradition. The political culture of the 1960s, which was promoted across the continent by the infamous CEPAL (Economic and Political Commission for Latin America), had permeated Peruvian policy in the hands of the military. The philosophy it preached, under the guise of impressive-sounding names such as structuralism and anti-imperialism, was economic nationalism, import substitution, state industrialization, expropriation, and, in general, an understanding of economic relations with the world as a kind of revenge against the supposed historical looting our republics had been subjected to following that other great historical looting, colonialism.

To this philosophy, shared in Latin America by both the left and the right, from Allende to Perón, the Peruvian military added a marked socialist slant under the influence of a sector of Peruvian communism linked mainly with the Moscow line. Communist penetration in the military government was never complete; however, it was seriously tainted by the political philosophy of the times. Not even with the Morales Bermúdez coup against Velasco Alvarado, which brought about a supposed break with the socialist inclinations of the first military phase, did the essence of the implanted system change. As a result of the wide diffusion of this political mentality, in the 1980s Peruvian democracy was in the hands of political parties maintaining old ideas from the 1950s and 1960s because of the hibernation into which a dozen years of military rule had forced them. They had made no mental transition regarding modern forms of understanding international relations, the causes of poverty, and the keys to prosperity. The governments of Belaunde and Alan García, then, did not dare to privatize a single one of the more than 200 public enterprises created by the military rulers, which had ruined strong mining and fishing sectors. Nor did they touch the cooperatives, which had replaced the private *haciendas* in the countryside and which, in the hands of politicized and incompetent bureaucrats, had ruined agriculture even more. By 1990 state parasitism was affecting a million and a half Peruvians and their families. Rules and regulations, corruption, and a proliferation of state bodies had placed a padlock on the country's capacity for progress. The system inherited from the military dictatorship had been essentially preserved by the democratic governments.

But there were other forms of military pressure on democracy, which had to do with the struggle against the combined threat of drug trafficking and terrorism. It was the worst thing that could happen to an emerging democracy faced with the tremendous task of starting from zero with the rebuilding of civilian institutions that would, through a wide consensus, place power under tolerant, respected, and legitimate forms of institutional life, and faced, equally, with the need for serious reform in the society it had inherited. That inheritance was a combination of the old ills of the republic (centralism, mercantilism, and social disintegration and breakup) and those of the military period (authoritarianism, populism, and state control). In essence, all this required a formidable promotion of the individual into a national life that, until then, had been in the hands of the state, or those in collusion with it, and had hindered widespread participation in the affairs of the nation and social mobility. It was a grave error of the democratic governments not to seize the time when they could to carry out such changes in the republic. This, in the final analysis, would offer ammunition to the enemies of the democratic system to blame democracy itself, and not the governments making use of it, for the disasters.

This is the context in which *Sendero Luminoso* made its apocalyptic appearance. Among the many traumas it provoked in Peruvain democracy was its confrontation with civilian institutions, posing a challenge to which the democratic government gradually gave in, turning things over to the military. The opportunity came for the military class, which after the return to democracy had drawn back in shame and defeat, to return to center stage on the national political scene. This was much less evident, of course, in the capital than in the provinces during the first half of the 1980s, but in the long run it was clear throughout the country. Unlike most other things in Peru, the subversive challenge of *Sendero Luminoso* and the militarization process linked with it were both decentralized phenomena moving strongly from the outside into the capital itself.

Sendero Luminoso began its war in May 1980 with an attack on an electoral college in the remote town of Chuschi in the Peruvian Andes. But its existence as such came earlier. It was a movement that emerged in the Andean department (state) of Ayacucho in the 1960s among a group of provincial *mestizos,* a social class especially resentful about the virtual prostration of the Andean. Due to economic growth in those years, they had gained a social and political consciousness that was lacking on the part of their Andean neighbors, groups of Peruvian peasants of which their fathers and grandfathers were often a part.

Abimael Guzmán, a philosophy professor at the University of San Cristóbal de Huamanga in the Andean city of Ayacucho and who had graduated with a thesis on Kant, formed, at the beginning of the 1960s, an Ayacucho regional committee of the Communist party, and soon began to organize a faction. So during the radical division in 1964 between pro-Moscow and pro-Beijing sectors, in accordance with developments on the international scene, Guzmán's faction opted for Maoism. That began a long march toward ideological purity that resulted in a great deal of push and pull among the Maoists themselves. In 1970, with his base always at the University of San Cristóbal de Huamanga, Guzmán was ousted from the Communist party and formed his own Communist party, the *Sendero Luminoso*.

Under the military dictatorship in the 1970s, there was a growing political and ideological cohesion among members, an expansion of activities in Ayacucho, and a great debate regarding the option of armed struggle in that world (the Andes) against the state, which, despite its socialist pretenses, was named as the exploiter. So there emerged the fascinating and fatal process of the sharp radicalization of the left, with *Sendero Luminoso* as the most extreme expression of it (but at that point, not the only one). It was a radicalization egged on to a large degree by Velasco's "socialist revolution," the cooperation of the pro-Moscow Communist party with the government, and the need for a series of political movements to distance themselves from the central administration, be it for ideological reasons, frustrations in their ranks regarding popular backing for reforms under way, or the impossibility of coming to power. In his travels to China, Guzmán came to admire the decade of the Cultural Revolution and, though he did not get to know Mao personally (he managed only once to see him from afar), he was in tune with his crusade.

The peak of *Sendero* fanaticism came in 1976 with the death of Mao, the defeat of the "gang of four" led by Mao's widow, and with the demise of the spirit of the Cultural Revolution. From that moment on Guzmán and *Sendero*, moved by something of a mystical sense of ideological purpose, took on the responsibility of shoring up the Maoist revolution and becoming world guides for a Communist movement betrayed by all Communist power centers on earth. So *Sendero* began to take on the aspect of a messianic, quasi-religious, movement. This, together with the radicalization process of the Peruvian left (of which it was a part) which was frustrated with the growing disparity between rhetorical reform and practical results, pushed the grouping toward armed struggle. Beginning in 1980, all of this was put in the service of a Maoist "peoples war" from the countryside to the city.

To a large extent, *Sendero* is heir to the catastrophe of the military government of the 1970s under whose very eyes it grew and armed itself systematically and ruthlessly in preparation for its mad crusade. Unlike what might have been expected, the failure of Socialist reform did not demoralize groups like *Sendero*. On the contrary, it provided its ideology with better grounds for fanatical pursuit and brought home something

that its members were denouncing on the international scene: th
of most self-proclaimed Socialist and Communist movements of the
world. Furthermore, it reinforced the hatred against the state, which was
at the core of its convictions and which constituted a very powerful
weapon of persuasion among the provincial mestizos resentful of their
own low social status.

This is the group that in 1980 opened fire on democracy. Faced with
this opposition, the democratic government opted in the first years to do
nothing. Understandably, it didn't want to order the troops to leave the
barracks. Less understandably, it dismissed *Sendero*'s actions as mere
"fireworks." The growth of *Sendero* in those years in the Ayacucho zone
and in several neighboring Andean provinces, isolated propaganda
coups, and criminal actions in the capital created a climate of tension,
which, in view of the weaknesses or incompetence of democratic ad-
ministrations, made it necessary to return the center of Peruvian political
life to the military. That is the beginning of the story that ended on 5 April
1992 with a coup d'état by Alberto Fujimori and the military apparatus.
Sendero, of course, is not responsible for the return of the military. But
it became, in time—especially as a result of the growing awareness of
civilian incapacity—a catalyst of the military comeback, together with
drug trafficking. The military was there before the 1980 attack on
Chuschi, with its long antidemocratic tradition, its sense of political
mission, and its hierarchic organization. Conversely, civilian institutions
lacked the will power, organization, cohesion, and authority to build a
democracy.

Between 1982 and 1989, more and more areas of Peru fell into the
hands of the military, where so-called emergency zones were under the
absolute control of military-political commandos. The Belaunde government created the first such zone in 1982. It encompassed several provinces in the departments of Ayacucho and Apurímac, both in the southern
Peruvian Andes. The second was on the edge of the jungle. Political life
in Lima continued on a democratic plane. From the beginning, there were
denunciations against the acts of these political-military commandos,
which were aired in the press and investigated by Parliament; but where
things were taking place, microcosms of a military dictatorship were
functioning via the concept of emergency zones. They held complete
power and were the highest authority in the zone. They reported to the
civilian government in Lima, but the bulk of their decisions and actions

escaped civilian scrutiny; reports sent to the capital reflected only a tiny part of what was going on. Thus, the country became aware that there were important zones in the Andes where the Peruvian state did not exist, despite its suffocating presence elsewhere in the country. The arrival of the military in places where there had been no previous state existence, sparked by the presence of *Sendero* in or around those areas, opened the way to the establishment of military power; nothing had to be replaced in terms of legitimate civilian authority. There would simply be a state beginning at zero. Generals who were good and bad, authoritarian and tolerant, right wing and left wing, corrupt and less corrupt served in these political-military commandos. But when in 1988 the García government established an emergency zone in Junín, a department in the central Peruvian Andes, we were already faced with what, in practical terms, could be called a military government in eight Peruvian departments, a total extension of over 1,000 by 350 kilometers; that is, a third of the national territory. During this period, there were a number of times when Lima lived under a state of emergency, and during the first year and a half of the Fujimori government (that is, during his democratic period) that was almost always the situation in Lima. The state of emergency meant the suspension of a number of constitutional rights in the capital.

The department of Junín, which in 1988 was added to the list of emergency zones, is a strategic area for Peru. The Mantaro Valley, thanks to a hydroelectric plant, is the source of most of the energy used in the capital and part of the Peruvian coast. Links between this area and Lima are decisive for food supplies. When at the end of the 1980s *Sendero Luminoso*, as part of its Maoist design to approach the city from the countryside, made this department one of its strategic points, the military was forced a number of times to supply the capital by helicopters. This offers some idea of the power being assumed in those years by the military establishment, which began to control the key department of Junín. The power of the military was unlimited, and its use of that power was broad. This had a twofold effect: state violence and the absence of success against the real enemy. In 1984 in La Mar province in Ayacucho 10 percent of the adult peasant population (around 100,000 people) were wiped out by the military response to *Sendero Luminoso*. Suffice it to say that *Sendero* has continued to grow since then and still exists in that corner of the Andes.

But we cannot understand the magnitude of the degenerative Maoist subversion brought to the democratic society of the 1980s without stressing its similarities with another sort of subversion of institutional order: drug dealing. Our burgeoning democracy became powerless in the face of this virus, which would quickly spread throughout the world of power in Peru. It is not the use of drugs that helps drug dealing weaken democracy. This is a minor aspect with which any new or old democratic society can deal. Far more serious, in a society where the activity is illegal, is its ability to penetrate, grow, and remain within the institutional bodies. It is also an alternative power that surreptitiously supplants democratic power and neutralizes any possibility of creating solid institutions.

The drug business was not invented in 1979, when democracy was about to begin. It was during the military rule of the 1970s that coca plantations increased fivefold, revealing a growing demand[3]. But it was only during the 1980s that the coca business really mushroomed. It is calculated that between 200 and 300 thousand families are involved in the coca zones, mainly in the valley of the Alto Huallaga. They sow and harvest coca over an area of around 300,000 hectares. During the 1980s Peru came to provide 65 percent of the raw material for the world market. While coca gave Peru about $1 billion (some statistics indicate $ 2 billion) annually, and so played a crucial role in easing the economic crisis, it sparked and organized a power apparatus that would prove deadly for the survival of the democratic system. In the mid-1980s the Alto Huallaga Valley saw an aggressive penetration of *Sendero Luminoso*, which had discovered a way to finance its murderous ideological undertaking through an organization in the zone, the essence of which was the receipt of money in exchange for the protection of coca dealers and drug barons. This has guaranteed them some $ 60 million a year, a sum infinitely higher than the total finances of legal political parties in Peru during the twelve years between the return to democracy in 1980 and the coup in April 1992.

Faced with this alliance, the Peruvian government responded as always: the zone surrounding Río Huallaga was put in the hands of the military. In this case, the military was forced to cooperate with the anti-narco police beginning to operate regularly in the region with the growing help of the DEA (U.S. Drug Enforcement Agency) from a base at Santa Lucía, built with American aid and set in motion in 1989 following the announcement of the Andean strategy of George Bush. The policy of the military in the Huallaga zone from 1984 to the 1990s fluctuated between an emphasis on combating *Sendero*, which meant gaining confidence among the coca growers and their intermediaries (that is, tolerance for cultivation and then for sales), and a strong repression of drugs, following the line of the anti-narco police. This meant several things, among them, the participation of a huge number of Peruvian officers and functionaries in the coca network and the resources it was mining. It also meant the undermining of institutional order, Peruvian democracy, and an important concentration of military power. It doesn't matter that from 1984, when General Carvajal took over the emergency zone encompassing Alto Huallaga, to 1992, more than six generals fell, thanks to denunciations or outright incompetence in their missions. The final result is that the military and political apparatus in the zone—which survived upheavals at the top brought about by denunciations from the capital, where a democratic system was still in effect—became an integral part of that system, carrying out the double role of providing Peru the greater part of its income and undermining the foundations of civilian institutions.

Besides, while becoming a decisive power in a zone offering *Sendero* the bulk of its resources, the dependence of the democratic state on the military grew progressively greater, like drug addiction. No charges of human rights violations or of complicity with the drug traffic—such as those made before the U.S. Senate at the end of the 1980s by Melvyn Levitsky, assistant secretary for International Narcotics Matters against General Arciniegas, who was in charge of the zone for several months—made any difference. There was in place a system of variable alliances, desired or not, among the three powers in the zone: the military, the narcos, and *Sendero*. It was an evil circle and an essentially fixed system. The alliance between the military and the coca dealers could not destroy *Sendero*, nor could making the fight against drugs a priority (between 1986 and 1987, for example), and therefore giving less attention to *Sendero*, diminish drug dealing. Peru's democratic state and its civilian institutions, meanwhile, were completely apart from this world, which was coming to rule the country's destiny.

The economic policy directed from Lima by the democratic government during the second half of the 1980s had a decisive influence on this state of affairs. Agrarian policy meant a tough price control aimed at benefiting the consumer, while it fomented a fiscal imbalance that would bring on a serious inflation rate, dissolving the mirage of reduced prices. But most affected by this policy during the Alan García government (1985-90) was the farmer, the peasant, whose cultivated products were scarcely profitable and the sale of which, in many cases, did not meet costs, leaving him with no chance of conquering a market for himself. As if this were not enough, the government, obsessed with following the Keynesian line of stimulating demand in the industrial field, wanted to consolidate the lowering of consumer prices on foodstuffs (apart from price controls) via food imports with which the crippled farmers simply could not compete. All the other areas of the economy—in line with the old Latin American tradition of "defense against foreign economic aggression"—were strongly protected. This created an imbalance between the countryside and the city even greater than that which the democratic government had inherited.

Thus, coca was the only profitable crop, the peasant's only defense in the face of the calamity with which Lima had struck the countryside. The agrarian reform of the military government had been a disaster and the democratic government finished it off. The agrarian situation resulting from the clumsiness of the democratic government is reflected in the fact that in 1990 Peruvian peasants shared 15 percent less of the national income than five years before. Among other consequences of these errors, the expansion of coca in the Alto Huallaga zone led to the development of a completely coca-oriented economy, where the military apparatus as well as *Sendero* played key roles.

The relationship of forces between the capital, where civilians ruled, and the interior, which was the realm of the military, was changing, as was the situation among the military of the capital itself. The function of the military in the capital was no longer that of bringing the military in the interior into line with a democratic system of which they were a part in Lima. Sensitive to the antidemocratic magnetism coming from the emergency zones that, like in the Huallaga, were the key to Peruvian life, the military in Lima aimed rather to promote the power structure in the emergency zones and the provinces in general. So there emerged an interweaving of interests around this state of affairs that could be said to be national in magnitude. Violence, of course, had left off being a remote feature of the country's interior. The presence of *Sendero* in Lima began very early and was graphically illustrated by those dogs hanging from lamp posts with posters denouncing the "dog" Deng Xiao Ping. But, it was not until later, in the middle of the first half of the decade, that *Sendero Luminoso* began to make clear inroads in the capital. The effect was, little by little, to bring to Lima, the seat of political decisions and of the political class in general, many of the characteristics that violence had sparked in the countryside. One of these was the strengthening, beyond the natural role within the democratic system, of military involvement. June 1986 saw the massacre of 256 *Sendero* militants who had staged a riot in Lima prisons. Alan García had given in to the military, and the latter showed they were ready to take seriously their new place in the new power structure in the capital without much concern for the domestic or foreign organizations watching over them.

Democracy was being eroded by a slow degradation of the notions of authority, of the preeminence of civilian values, and of the order stemming from the recent (1979) Constitution. Violence was coming not only from the *Sendero* people; the multiple sources of violence were a distinct feature of the new state of affairs and a powerful symbol of the gradual disintegration of state authority. In 1984 the *The Tupac Amaru Revolutionary Movement (MRTA) was born*. It took its name from the famous Indian who had rebelled against colonial rule in the eighteenth century. Its main goal was to revive the failed guerrilla adventures of the 1960s along Castroist lines. This group operated in the interior, primarily in the jungle zone of San Martín and also in Alto Huallaga. But its presence in Lima had a profound psychological impact; there it was involved in a wave of kidnappings of wealthy Peruvian businessmen, for which extremely high ransoms were demanded. By contrast with *Sendero*, which was financed by coca, the *Tupac Amaru* people received their foreign aid from Latin American communism. But it wasn't enough. This is why they chose to kidnap businessmen. The move was devastating for the morale of the wealthy.

In response, the business class opted for a costly private protection service, and in a short period of time Lima saw a proliferation of private security services and easy access to arms. A good part of these companies were made up of retired policemen or former members of the military. The growth of private armies was of great influence during the breakdown in central authority. At the same time, the military region of Lima saw a strengthening of the power of its officers responsible for military mobilization, above all in the late 1980s, due to successive declarations of a state of emergency in the capital and to various curfews, following the model already established throughout the country. In addition to all this, around 1988—as a response to the inefficiency of the judicial system in dealing with captured insurgents—there appeared in Lima the *Rodrigo Franco Commando*. It was egged on by a sector of the APRA party deeply involved in the interior ministry, the leadership of which has been attributed to the man who was then minister.

In this crossfire of armed movements, civilian democracy quickly began to lose authority in the country and among its adherents. First, there was the *Sendero Luminoso* with various organizations structured under the "Movement in Defense of the Peoples Revolution," which included everything from a group charged with working its way into the trade unions along the Carretera Central de Lima (key to the capital's industrial life) to a movement responsible for penetrating into the shantytowns surrounding metropolitan Lima. Then, there was the *Rodrigo Franco Commando* with its attacks on people linked to the terrorists and its threats against government opposition. Even we in the independent *Libertad* movement received such threats. Next, there was the *Tupac Amaru* threat. Its effectiveness as a terrorist organization was far less than that of *Sendero*, but it demolished the faith of the Peruvian business class in the democratic regime and the institutional life it might provide. Finally, we had the armed forces. They had been pushed aside by a democratic exuberance in 1980 after the debacle of their leadership of the Peruvian government, but now their presence in the capital was advancing in giant leaps. It wasn't nearly as powerful as in the interior, but it was obviously dangerous to a country that was in the business of taking, or failing to take, painful steps toward civilian institutions of consensus. Between 1987 and 1990 Amnesty International designated Peru as the country with most human rights violations and the highest number of missing people. In 1990 the U.S. Senate blocked the granting of some $100 million in military aid requested by the White House on behalf of Peru, in light of atrocities committed by the armed forces.

This is the context in which the 1990 electoral campaign developed. The Democratic Front coalition, led by my father, believed it was making the last great effort to rescue the civilian option in Peru on behalf of the democratic system that had emerged in 1980, in whose immense possibilities a large number of Peruvians still had confidence. The climate of banditry that had invaded the capital, the proliferation of small "states" or parallel powers, a culture of "nonofficial" arms, and the ethic of violence in civilian as well as military human relations had taken control in Peru by 1990. Toward the end of the center-right Belaunde government (1980-85), when political disorder rather than economic crisis gave the people the perception of a government with feet of clay not worthy of their respect, the Alan García option had emerged. Its progressive image promised to block the return of the military, which was being called for in many Peruvian sectors. At the end of the left-wing García government (1985-90), rumors of a military coup were again rampant. But this time, added to the chaos and the sinking of the country into a state that was more Fourth World than Third, there was the old tendency of the APRA party to authoritarianism, intolerance, and trickery, of which the president was frequently guilty. He had tried state control of the financial system with an eye to bringing down the press, controlling the finances of all private economic practice and thereby remaining in power. A large mobilization of Peruvians had blocked his plans and at the same time signaled the beginning of the end of the president's honeymoon with the people, as well as cutting off any general's plans for taking over the country amid the national demoralization. The *Libertad* movement, born from the protest against the García government, had acted as a bulwark against a military coup. By 1990 the country was in agony. It was not hard to see that the popular rejection of politicians was dangerously confused with a lack of confidence in the democratic system; and it was obvious that this was the interpretation that could be easily offered by broad sectors of the military. This is the reason we took on a political campaign headed by a writer who, despite having spent his life involved in political debate, was a complete stranger to the political business of struggling for power. My father took personal risks, suffered two murder attempts, received a multitude of death threats, stood up to physical confrontations with government thugs, and engaged in debates that degenerated into insults and petty intrigues. Throughout these difficulties, he tried to convince Peruvians that a serious reform based on a market economy offering the greatest access to the instruments of wealth (which had historically been controlled by a minority closely linked to the state) was the only way to stop the barbarity toward which the country was headed—the end of the democratic system.

What was not then known was that a complex military apparatus embedded in the Intelligence Service was already preparing such an option. This group was implanted in the fertile fields of Peru's crisis under democracy and astutely waited for its chance. The opportunity appeared, of course, with this civilian coming out of the blue: Alberto Fujimori. He had no structure of his own and no plans for governing. He was desperately in need of organization when it came to the second round in the electoral battle. Up to then his *état majeur* had been a vague collection of leftists who intuitively felt that the political moment favored the independent image that Fujimori had nurtured for himself and had come onto him with proposals that were essentially negative. They rejected the Democratic Front's plans to defeat inflation, to privatize public enterprizes, to push forward commercial liberalization, to engage the mobilization of civilian society against terrorism, to offer land titles to peasants in the cooperatives and the Andean and costal communities, and a vast state reform in order to return its authority, and take away from it much of its dead weight with an end to restoring its essential role, that of an impartial guarantor of a market economy.

The Intelligence Service approached Fujimori when Vladimiro Montesinos saw in Fujimori's legal problems opportunities to climb higher on the ladder of power. None of this came out during the campaign, but it became more and more evident from the moment the man took office. His connections with the military establishment were extensive, powerful and surprising: in a short period of time he was living at the "Pentagonito," the army general headquarters, something not even Velasco of Morales Bermúdez had dared to do. The confirmation of this structural relationship came on 28 July, the date he officially took power, when there began a series of radical changes in the military hierarchy, which I have already mentioned. The boldness with which these changes were carried out is explained by the presence of former Captain Montesinos in the background. So, while the Intelligence Service became more autonomous and important, the top military authorities were politically indebted to Montesinos and to a large extent came under the thumb of the intelligence community.

This slow taking of power was more than exclusively military in tone. An essential part of the strategy was civilian and consisted of the change Fujimori underwent, beginning with the first days of his government, regarding his political line up to then. It was evident to his advisers that the times had changed decisively and that the reforms the Democratic Front had demanded from the other end of the field were not only the best way of avoiding the disintegration of Peru, but the *only* way. To a certain extent, the previous decades had left the man in power with the *obligation* of taking on the difficult task of breaking with political, social, economic, and even cultural tradition in the country. What remained to be seen was to what degree and how fast. But it was clear that the road the Democratic Front had pointed out—echoing what was for some overwhelmingly obvious and was beginning to be so even for Peru's most stubborn—was the only one for a country suffering an 8,000 percent annual inflation rate, a bankrupt state, and a civilian society angry with and scornful of official institutions.

For me, one of the most fascinating aspects of the campaign is that those of us who lost ended up winning, subtly and quietly, the consciousness of almost the entire Peruvian political class that was fighting us. In 1988, when we entered the political campaign for the 1990 elections, soon after the mobilizaton of *Libertad* against the government's attempt at capturing the financial system, the Peruvian political class, both left and right, was clinging to the old standbys of Peruvian life: nationalism, populism, state control, the culture of subsidy, mercantilism, and statism. Although they all thought they were mortal enemies, the different parties, pressure groups, political institutions, mass media, and those forming public opinion in general made up part of a model that they, from their different positions, had helped to create.

The campaign for the 1990 elections saw an incredible ideological turn in the history of Peru. The Democratic Front's program was made public in December 1989 at an annual meeting of businessmen and executives (CADE), the forum traditionally used by those aspiring to power to present their platforms. That program quickly became the only item on the agenda. The electoral battle revolved exclusively around it, while the adversaries of the Democratic Front worked out strategies to demolish it with a careful and systematic distortion of all its proposals. The shock therapy associated with the initial stages of monetary stabilization designed to stop inflation became part of the political demonology of the nation and was presented as a great conspiracy to wipe away 500,000 jobs, kill old people and children of hunger, crush the savings of the middle class, and make the cost of services skyrocket. The plans to follow the stabilization—state reforms limiting ministries and the bureaucracy, cutting down on regulations and interference in the business sector, spreading stock ownership, and slashing the cost of enterprise—

were also pictured as a grand plan of the powerful to ruin Peru. The proposal of mobilizing civilian society against terrorism and stimulating peasant and worker self-defense, which the Democratic Front defended, was inspired vaguely by the example of President Betancourt in Venezuela in the 1960s. He had managed to head a successful response to Communist terrorism by putting the bulk of the responsibility on the civilian population, at a time when fighting guerrilla activity took a lot of political courage. This was presented as opting for a generalized civil war and promoting the use of violence. Reforms in education offering free services only to those unable to pay and using the money saved to improve the infrastructure was played up as an effort to block the right of needy people to schooling, despite our emphasis on education as a powerful instrument, the best one, in the long-term redistribution of the country's wealth, as long as the state stayed away from it as much as possible.

We believed that our considerable advantage in the polls reflected a strong popular consciousness regarding the reasons for poverty in Peru and what is key to creating wealth; and we stood behind this in our ongoing promise to make Peru "a country of property owners and businessmen." Even our advisers from the U.S. consulting firm Sawyer and Miller wrote reports to campaign headquarters assuring us that "C and D are discussing liberal ideas" (C and D referred to the poorest sectors of the electorate), which, in effect, seemed to be the case.

But even more interesting was the fact that other candidates and parties, desperate to destroy the libertarian program, had more or less unconsciously assimilated several of these lessons concerning the republican failure in Peru and refused to defend the old ideological archetypes, the old political labels whose truths had been left empty by the terrible Peruvian decadence. There was emerging a vague political consensus that was then hard to detect behind the wave of dogfights in the campaign but that we, influenced by my father's uphill struggle to make the elections a massive plebiscite on the ideas of freedom, looked upon with fascination. At times it seemed as if we were the government and our adversaries the opposition. There was nothing else on the table to talk about. The virulence of the attacks made for an atmosphere of a project under way, even that of a government in power. This led many to believe that the Peruvian people were beginning to take on the features of liberal thought and action.

What Fujimori's victory demonstrated, of course, was that we were wrong, that the adhesion to our proposal was, as often happens in these cases, instinctive, emotional, and not the product of a firm ideological conviction. But it also showed that the Peruvian people had cast aside the country's old political forms. The defenders of those forms—even though they had downplayed their old beliefs during the campaign, foreseeing the success we might have in our attempt to create a liberal ideology among the electorate—did not fare well. APRA, together with the Marxist left, which five years earlier had won over almost two-thirds of the electorate and had moved the center right out of central and local power, were now reduced to only one-fourth of the votes. The remainder of the ballots, cast for Vargas Llosa and Fujimori, sent a curious message. The electorate had understood the reasons for the national disaster and opted for change. But there was an almost visceral lack of confidence in radical or abrupt change. Peruvians are Peruvians, resigned and patient beneath that gray sky of the capital, where a third of the population lives perennially halfway between the light of day and the dark of night. Fujimori had said only what he planned *not* to do, being careful as well to attack the *status quo*. So Peruvians voted for the Democratic Front and Cambio 90, in what amounted to the consensus that we had detected in the campaign, but were unable to capitalize on. The people had understood the republic's disaster, but they had not accepted the proposal of an explicit change, they preferred a vague and lukewarm program with no definite silhouette.

It was in this context that Fujimori took power and launched, in the face of all predictions, an economic stabilization plan tougher than what could have been imagined. The suspicions were confirmed. The 1990 electoral campaign had rooted in Peru a rather modern and liberal political culture oriented to state austerity and the incorporation of more citizens into the market economy, something that, with some variations, seemed to be the case across Latin America. There were essential differences, however, between the program applied by the government and the one put forward by the Democratic Front. Essentially, we had proposed action regarding reforms to take place almost simultaneously with measures against inflation in order to combat an inevitable recession. We had foreseen what the specialists call an exchange "overshooting," fixing the exchange rate temporarily at a stable rate after devaluation so that the immediate liberalization of trade would find industrialists with better defenses against imports, since the latter would become even more expensive; the exporters could benefit from the exchange rate by reacting immediately, while the state could reap profits from taxes. So once the situation was stabilized, we would have left exchange completely unfettered in an atmosphere of free trade. It was a case of extenuating the blow of shock therapy in those crucial first days and avoiding the crippling effect the measures would otherwise have on the nation's economic forces.

The Fujimori government did not do this, and its measures brought about an unprecedented recession in Peru, which two and a half years later was not even slightly reduced. The coup d'état on 5 April 1992, contributed, along with a serious wound to economic agents, to a conversion of this recession into an almost endemic trait of the Peruvian economy. The data is eloquent. Inflation was lowered to 60 percent per year, tremendous news for a country that in 1990 had an inflation rate bordering on 8,000 percent. The accumulated reserves of the government came to $2 billion, thanks to the collection of taxes, which Peruvians have always tried to avoid. But tragically, their project bubbled over and suffocated an economy that was already stymied. Ninety percent of the small and middle-level mining firms, on which the Peruvian economy heavily depended, were closed down. Ninety percent of the textile enterprises, geared to export, went bankrupt. Banks, savings and loans institutions, the biggest supermarket chains, and dozens of other important businesses collapsed. The paralysis has cost Peru some $4 billion in national income.

It is important to note that the orientation of the economic program has been in contradiction to Peru's recent history, thanks in part to that strange consensus emerging from the polemic of 1990 and the reality Fujimori found when he came to power. The suspicion, however, that this kind of policy was not born out of conviction but out of a short-term need to satisfy the International Monetary Fund and build up the nation's coffers so as to go back to old policies came in January 1993, when Fujimori's minister of economics resigned his post, denouncing the government's return to populism. Feeling secure with the small amount of reserves the country had been able to accumulate, the dictatorship—conscious that the only way to prevent a strike from the constitutionalist sector of the army in a bid to return to the rule of law was to keep high scores in the polls—began once again to throw money away.

But there is also a third factor allowing us to understand the power structure that was lurking in the background from the second round in the elections to the establishment of the dictatorship in 1992: the military. This group was for thirty years Peru's major trustee of the failed political philosophy of economic nationalism, a growth of the state in regard to "strategic necessities," the substitution of imports and correlated protectionism, and the kind of Third World philosophy born after the end of World War II among recently independent colonies, where Marxism seemed to have moved while it was wilting in the prosperous West and which later spread to Latin America, the Western periphery.

Today we can see how these same military people—at least broad sectors of the armed forces—have begun to take on, just like the civilians, new notions concerning the Peruvian state and society emerging from the 1990 electoral campaign. It was a fragile realization, which might fall apart in the face of a prolongation of difficulties with economic plans. There is no other way to explain the active participation, right from the beginning, of the military establishment in the government program, where Fujimori renounced all his electoral promises. This is especially true of those military men who, crouching in the Intelligence Service, were planning their grab for power. Up to that point, it was customary for the leaders of the Peruvian Marxist left to parade at the Center for High Military Studies (CAEM). Many of them, as well as those listening to them, had been an integral part of the military dictatorship of the 1970s, along with many researchers and professors from institutes and universities who until then seemed to have a monopoly on national academic life. At some imprecise moment, these officers listening to CAEM talks must have begun to close their ears to what was coming from the podium and open them to another sort of discourse taking root in their consciousness and coming from the outside. Possibly in secret, at night under the blanket, they read speeches, books, and pamphlets put out by the Democratic Front. A substantial part of the military establishment began to go along with the political consensus invading the country's official institutions and, to a lesser extent, more by intuition than analysis, so did many poorer Peruvians.

Other lessons had contributed to this new vision among the Peruvian military. The case of Chile was one of them. The Chilean case was the antithesis of the Peruvian situation of the 1970s. For the first time in Latin America, a country had managed to overcome the ineffectiveness and corruption of a military dictatorship via a model, based always on brute force and the absence of the rule of law, able to reconcile the military with economic efficiency and a more ethical behavior. The Chilean example was one of a military dictatorship that, throughout the 1980s, placed the economy in the hands of professionals who had graduated from American universities (mainly Chicago), believers in the blessings of free markets and the need to give a serious push to private enterprise. Their achievements were by no means insignificant: exports totaling almost $7 billion a year; a 54 percent growth between 1984 and 1992 (while the average growth in Latin America in the 1980s was scarcely 1.6 percent); an increase of the middle class, the engine of a capitalist economy; and fairly healthy state finances.

There were also many less striking areas of the economy and great social divisions, along with the perseverance, in many cases, of the scourge of state control. The copper mines, one of Chile's major sources of income, were kept in state hands, owing, no doubt, to the principle of "strategic necessity," and a percentage of the income therefrom was assigned to the military establishment, in what amounted to a huge subsidy. Although the reforms had taken a generation to germinate—and as late as 1982 Chile was known on the continent as the classic example of the failure of military dictatorships—the creation of a market economy without the labyrinth of obstacles existing in the rest of the Latin American countries soon proved to be a rapid and effective mechanism. To a great extent, the widespread repression was responsible for smothering the social agitation that inevitably emerges as a result of the dislocation always produced in a society moving toward a full market economy. The image of the Chilean military dictatorship had an impact on the Peruvian military, and I think on the military of other countries as well. I believe it was a decisive factor in the slow mental transformation that they all underwent at the beginning of the 1990s, away from the populist ethos that had dominated military thinking during the previous decades. But it was not a conversion to the liberal philosophy that Chile had undertaken, thanks in part to the fact that the military had decided not to become involved in the management of social and political policy. Tragically, it was a fascination with the totality of the model: the wedding of a military dictatorship with a free economy. What seeped into the Peruvian military consciousness was the association between strong government and economic liberalism, which a number of governments had practiced in recent years, not only in Latin America but also in Asia. There was, without our knowledge and probably without their realization, a growing fascination among the Peruvian military with the right wing model of Suharto in Indonesia and Lee Kuang Kew in Singapore, in place of the socialist militarism of Burma and, to a lesser extent, Bangladesh, which recent Latin American military mentality had quite distinctly echoed.

Another foreign situation also influenced the Peruvian military: the Argentinian example. In very hushed tones many Peruvian officers admired the generals who, between 1976 after the coup against Isabel Perón and 1983 when Raúl Alfonsín came to power via the electoral route, had used the government they had taken over to fight against subversion, believing that only indiscriminate repression could do away with Marxist urban guerrillas. This is a well-known story. The generals ruling Argentina during the second half of the 1970s were forced to face a half-guerrilla, half-terrorist movement led by the *Montonero* chief, Julio Firmenich. On the other side of the border the Uruguayan generals had to deal with the *Tupamaros*, a similar threat. In response to the challenge, the Argentinian military unleashed acts of repression that permeated all of society. It jailed thousands, killed thousands more, and set off a social psychosis from which the country is only now beginning to recover. The result was an almost organic fear of power on the part of civilian society. All these horrors are laid out in the report of a commission headed by writer Ernesto Sábato. The report backed up celebrated court cases where the democratic government tried five generals who had ruled the country during those years along with a series of high-ranking and middle-level officers. Those generals went to jail, while lower-ranking officers were favored by the amnesty decreed by the Raúl Alfonsín government sometime later. It was meant as a balanced solution, but it did not soften what was really a traumatic transition; in 1987, there was a military revolt that the people and leaders loyal to the government of the Radical party stopped in time. Later, Alfonsín's successor, Carlos Menem, would also have to face the destabilizing aftermath of the democratic takeover with the rebellion of the *carapintada* officers.

The "Argentinian example" became controversial in Latin America and was a paradigm for understanding the struggle against Marxist insurgency responsible since the 1960s throughout the continent for a permanent political quagmire that knew no boundaries and had no respect for peaceful minds. While some abhorred the Argentinian way, others, who remained silent during 1985 and 1986 when Argentinian democracy chastised those responsible, began to develop the thesis that the best way of dealing with Latin American subversive movements was applying the same principle of "total war."

In Peru the main defender of the "Argentinian example" was General Luis Cisneros Vizquerra. They called him "the gaucho" because part of his military formation had taken place in Argentina. He had also been a minister under General Morales Bermúdez during the second phase of the military dictatorship of the 1970s and with Belaunde's democratic government; he then retired from active service, though not from participation in the political debate. In the face of the savage and bloody violence of *Sendero Luminoso*, he began to shout out for drastic solutions. It was an intelligent thesis that he defended, presented as a formula for combat on all fronts, including the political, social, and psychological, where the backbone of the undertaking, military repression, was covered over by other dimensions and seemed to be at the service of a serious effort to wipe out the social roots of all backing for the insurgents. While playing up this thesis, he was unreserved in his praise for the Argentinian experience, establishing all sorts of parallels. In the beginning, Cisneros, who spoke more freely than many colleagues because he was retired, didn't seem to carry much weight among military people. But this changed little by little.

Thus, another element to be drawn from the decade of the 1980s, in which civilian institutions in Peru gradually lost ground (moral and then physical) to the military, was that the military temperament, irritated by the brutality of the *senderistas*, became hardened and the defenders of the dirty war thesis gained more followers. A particular event had sparked a real trauma among the men in uniform: the killing in La Paz, Bolivia, of military attaché Vega Llona. He was not, of course, the only military man killed by terrorism. Given the climate of institutional degradation at the end of the 1980s, when the proliferation of armed gangs turned the country, including Lima, into an Armageddon, it is not hard to imagine why the disposition of the military men was changing. In any case, this was evidently happening. Key posts in the emergency zones were falling into the hands of those representing a military option in the face of terrorism. In one case, a general favoring a strongly civilian and social emphasis who had come to power in the Ayacucho emergency zone held his post only for a short time. Soon after, he had been replaced by a hard-line general.

It's important to distinguish between the feelings of the military regarding what was going on in the country and in what spirit they looked upon a government elected according to the Constitution. While the military leadership had a repressive impulse and nurtured the idea that only the military could carry out the complementary task of penetrating the sectors of society where subversion might flourish, coup-oriented action was not part of its mentality. The situation was ideal for the generals: with no need to remove an elected civilian from power, with all the consequences on the foreign and domestic fronts, the military went along taking control of those zones of power where, in the final analysis, the line followed by the state in its response to terrorism and drug dealing was decided. This allowed men like Vladimiro Montesinos to operate from 1990 in the background without showing their faces and without ever having to take responsibility for the social unrest generated by a clumsy and partial application of an economic plan that was doubtless along the lines of common sense and was very convenient in preparing the ground toward the open grabbing of power by the military when the time was ripe. The civilian government of Fujimori was perfect for the plan. Its responsibility was economic initiative. Everything else in the country was taking giant steps toward military rule, under the guide of Montesinos, who had made decisive hierarchical changes from the first day in his subtle weaving of a power network leading up to total control.

It is evident that civilian power embedded in the presidency and military power coexisted in a convenient organization allowing the country to operate with a democratic face. Sooner or later, however, the two powers would have to deal democracy the final blow, and there would emerge a form of unfettered authoritarian power in accordance with that vast network of created interests that included everything from the coca trade in the Alto Huallaga zone to the military administration in half the country. I don't believe that they had a fixed date, but merely a vague plan to be put into action at least two years before the president's term would finish according to the Constitution. What is clear is that as of 28 July 1990 one could see lines toward a convergent point. Fujimori, who was advised intelligently by Montesinos from the very beginnings of his government, took it upon himself to systematically discredit and cut apart civilian institutions that still, however weakly, blocked the way

between Constitutional and absolute power. It was the Parliament that
suffered most from this slaughter. Among the thousand paradoxes of
Peruvian politics at that time was that the very country that voted for a
president against the establishment also voted for dozens of incumbent
congressmen, in many cases making use of the preferential vote allowing
Peru to choose particular candidates from within a party list. What
resulted was a Parliament where Cambio 90, the government party, did
not have an absolute majority, which ironically was very beneficial to the
government strategy. Despite this Parliament, which gave Fujimori
extraordinary powers to rule by decree, in accordance with tradition,
during his first few weeks, it was easy to convince public opinion to be
prejudiced against it and that the politicians were blocking the
government's thrust for reform.

Other institutions were also ambushed, including judicial power,
where the president had tremendous influence. But since the Supreme
Court was in the hands of a number of members named by the preceding
government, the country was convinced that it was another of the
reactionary enclaves working against serious reform. Not even the
Catholic church hierarchy, with which Fujimori had had serious differences during the electoral campaign, was spared from ongoing criticism. It
was said to have a conservative mentality and to be suspicious of several
proposals regarding birth control. At first sight, all this seemed well and
good: a reformist going to the people demanding that decrepit institutions
opt for change. But in fact it was a subtle strategy designed to create a
climate in which these institutions, weakened in the face of public
opinion and trapped in their own bureaucratic conservatism, would lose
what little legitimacy they had left. The only institution never called into
question and never pointed to for the housecleaning it needed was, of
course, the armed forces.

The strategy of harassment and breaking down of civilian institutions
became more severe as the economic havoc became more permanent. At
the same time, the date of the coup drew closer, although there was no
specific timetable. For the fifth consecutive year, 1990 saw the Peruvian
economy falling—this time by 4 percent. But it was in the 1991-92 period
that the damaging effects of the economic plan were really felt. The
Peruvian economy continued to show no growth, and capital returning
from abroad (called "swallow capital" because of its tendency to fly off)
was weak. At the same time, resources leaving Peru to pay for imports

were far greater than the country's income. This meant a trade deficit of over $200 million. Inflation, the containment of which had been the only important achievement of the government, began to go up again in 1992. The interest rates were recessive, and suffocating exchange conditions for exports made it difficult for the country to react in the face of the healthy injection of foreign products entering the country. The effects on the government's popularity were being felt.

This is what was happening on the surface. But in the background the grabbing of power by a group of people not subject to legislative control or journalistic investigation, and some without even official government posts, was becoming more serious. Montesinos was not alone. There were others involved. Many of them were relatives of Fujimori whose names had never been mentioned during the 1990 electoral campaign and whose power center, working directly out of Government Palace, was responsible, over and above appointed ministers, for different areas of government competence. That power center was, of course, via Montesinos, who was also controlling the military. Montesinos was emerging as a kind of Peruvian Rasputin or Fouché. Aside from Montesinos, the president's brother, Santiago Fujimori, hand in hand with his wife, was the most powerful. The sister of the president, Rosa Fujimori, was also part of the inner circle of power. Although Santiago was officially a protocol attaché and Rosa was a private secretary, neither had responsibilities for which they were forced to account. But they were involved in everything, including the president's agenda, distributing donations coming from abroad, the naming of people to executive posts, preparations for foreign travel, and communications with the Casa de Pizarro (Presidential Palace). Many of these duties went beyond their nominal responsibilities.

In Montesinos's inner power circle directly involved in the Government Palace we find several figures as disreputable as Montesinos himself. There was Segisfredo Luza with his long history as a psychiatrist collaborating with military information services before the days of democracy, and who had been sent to jail after the murder of the husband of a patient who had consulted him in a case of severe depression. He had met Montesinos in prison, and was later set free with a presidential anmesty. Jorge Sosa Miranda, another mediocre former official of the Velasco military dictatorship, and Augusto Zimmerman, also a former communications secretary of the military dictatorship of the 1970s,

F gov undermined when wife denounces
family & re-selling clothes donated by ?

The Death of Democracy   39

rounded out the team. Under the orders of Montesinos they administered the propaganda and communications policy. In military and psychotechnical jargon this was termed "psycho-social politics." After the April 1992 coup the intelligence services managed to mobilize some 3,000 people following the orders of the political apparatus. Their scheming policies were already the real governing power in Peru between 1991 and 1992, before the coup. This power took on troubling dimensions, and little by little public opinion, not yet very well informed of its activities, began to ask questions.

There was a decisive event that offered Peru the chance to bring this behind-the-scenes governing into the open: it was the shocking corruption charges brought against Santiago Fujimori (the president's brother), his wife, and Rosa Fujimori (the president's sister), all members of the presidential family, by the First Lady, Susana Fujimori. The event ocurred on 24 March, after a trip to Japan by the president on which the First Lady did not go. The specific charges were that the people in question had used a large part of Japanese donations of used clothing for personal gain via resale. The scandal sparked off by this revelation played a decisive part in the coup d'état on 5 April that was planned by military intelligence advisers. In the climate of severe deterioration of the government's political strength, those charges set things off. Fujimori had recently been in Japan. There he had promised the Diet that he would return as president in the coming century. And while on a plane with a group of journalists and businessmen close to the regime, he discussed the possibility of forcing a confrontation with the Peruvian Parliament in order to win his hand. What was not made clear was that a coup d'état was coming. On his agenda, the final blow was probably set for a later date, allowing for the confrontation with Parliament to become more intense.

The first symptoms of the fact that Fujimori was going to push things ahead was that on his return from Japan he immediately paid a call on the "Pentagonito." He entered secretly by night in the military headquarters. Going against protocol, Fujimori appeared when the general commander of the army, Bari Hermoza, was not there to receive him. Meanwhile, a curious series of events took place among the rivals of the clan. On 25 March Fujimori asked the prosecutor, Víctor Cubas, to investigate the affair. On 26 March an unknown person laid charges against Fujimori and his wife, clearly in defense of Santiago Fujimori, whose power became quite evident in light of his ability to mobilize judges and lawyers ready to come face to face with Government Palace. On 27 March charges against the president and his wife were suddenly lifted. On 28 March the prosecutor announced, in turn, that Fujimori's brother was under no suspicion. On 1 April Susana Higushi moderated her charges before the prosecutor. It is clear that in the preceding forty-eight hours the family had made peace. What no one knew at that point was why things had happened so quickly.

Meanwhile, Parliament decided to ask for the formation of an investigatory commission to be named on 7 April. Fujimori had already decided that the democratic strategy must be speeded up. On 4 April he rejected the list of judges proposed by the judicial power to be ratified by the president. The coup came on 5 April. No investigatory commission was ever allowed to be formed.

Everything had been carefully prepared for the most appropriate day, and that day, 5 April, was decided by those particular circumstances. Montesinos had placed General José Valdivia in a key position: chief of the second military region, that is, head of the Lima armored division that would be in charge on 5 April of taking over centers of power and sending tanks to the streets. This man was the synthesis of the military spirit in control of the Fujimori/Montesinos strategy. While he was serving in the emergency zone he had been behind the notorious Cayara massacre where twenty peasants were killed by an Army patrol under his orders. After charges were laid against him following the Cayara massacre, witnesses had begun to disappear. Montesinos had taken responsibility for solving his legal problems and had assured him the top post when the time came to control the streets on the day of the coup. On the day of the coup, the tanks under Valdivia' s orders performed stupendously.

The military power structure that had been consolidated through the years surrounded Peruvian democracy with shocking swiftness during the Fujimori government. It was its responsibility to block and neutralize any civilian efforts from Lima to become involved in what the military considered its fiefdoms. This was the case, for example, of Hernando de Soto. He was an economist who had had some presidential aspirations and became one of Fujimori's advisers. He had shown some skill in working with any government, and had quite happily moved from being part of Alan García's team to serving Fujimori, who put him in charge of negotiations concerning the antidrug agreement between Peru and the United States and, more broadly, at the head of policy regarding the substitution of coca growing with other types of crops. He promised he could bring in more money from abroad with a strategy of reversing the Alan García tendency of breaking with the sources of international credit. Fujimori knew very well that the combat of drugs was the only way the U.S. might funnel important resources to Peru. This was, however, a surface picture. In the background, where things were really taking place, de Soto never had any real power. He failed in all his attempts to apply the policies that he had been named to enforce by his own chief. De Soto's letter of resignation (28 January 1992) is eloquent:

> the enemies of alternative development are one of the most subversive groups on the continent. . . and an important part of them are working for the State. The bullets which did away with Walter Costas, the first coca dealer to respond to the Presidential call for alternative development, came (according to members of his own trade) from the State. And drugs are sent out regularly from places controlled by the State.

(Hernando de Soto continued to act as an agent of Fujimori's de facto government, despite his resignation. The Peruvian weekly *Caretas* revealed, at the end of April 1993, the existence of a millionaire contract in dollars between his *Libertad y Democracia* think tank and Fujimori's government, in the purest mercantilist style. The pretext was rural property titles.)

The hand of Montesinos showed a decisive presence in the San Antonio, Texas, summit between the U.S. president and his colleagues from the Andean countries that export drugs or the raw materials for drugs. This was in February 1992. Fujimori's surprise charges of DEA corruption had an impact. They were, in fact, preventive charges. The DEA had in its possession devastating information on Montesinos. Toward the end of 1990 Montesinos had collaborated with the CIA (though it was not the first time he had done so). In 1991 the intelligence services under his control had begun the secret organization of an antidrug squad financed, recruited, and trained by the CIA. The DEA learned of Montesinos's résumé and was indignant. It privately released data on the relationship between Montesinos and the notorious Reynaldo Rodríguez López cartel. A 1991 report pointed out that Montesinos "had been successful in achieving the unconditional confidence of Fujimori and in becoming a friend of known drug dealers."[4] The CIA was very impressed with DEA proof that this antidrug entity it had helped finance and train never did its duty. As a consequence of this, Montesinos spoke out against the DEA in Lima in 1991, and months later in San Antonio, through the mouth of Fujimori, he struck again. There was the rumor (never confirmed) that the U.S. government had compiled a list of over 100 Peruvian military officers and officials directly implicated in the drug trade. Understandably, the antidrug agreements were blocked amid charges of corruption and human rights violations. The U.S. Congress froze military aid to Peru indefinitely. The day after the coup d'état "secret" information on what was behind this political-military intrigue in Peru began to circulate in the press around the world. In the United States Sam Dillon and Andrés Oppenheimer of the *Miami Herald* were the first to release the news.

This is how the slow process of the rotting of Peruvian democracy, begun twelve years before, resulted on 5 April 1992 in a coup in the form of a civilian dictator heading a military power apparatus. The vested interests of a powerful military sector and a furtive group closely linked to state leadership—where there was a mixture of everything from corruption and antidemocratic convictions to a simple lust for power—managed to smother a democracy that was gasping by 1992. The twelve years of democracy between 1980 and 1992 turned out not to be the "era" that we all called it, but a bend in the road, a digression after which everything—as poet Martín Adán said many years before, following a previous military coup—would return "to normal."

The taking of political power on 5 April 1992 by the military behind Fujimori was not in the least the beginning of a monolithic phase in the armed forces. There were no powerful reasons why the lack of institutional articulation affecting all of Peruvian life should have left the military untouched, although that body, owing to its corporate spirit, its history, and its political and economic stakes was less vulnerable to disintegration than the civilian world. As was made clear by the coup attempt against Fujimori and the army commander in chief, Nicola de Bari, at dawn on Friday, 13 November 1993, the military is not a monolith. It is a vast network of changing alliances, conflicting cliques, competing interests, and resentments harbored against specific influential people (Vladimiro Montesinos, for example) that at any moment might alter the hierarchy of power, but leave the military power structure as the basis of the new regime.

This "countercoup," in which many saw a maneuver by Montesinos and Fujimori to invent a movement of national and international solidarity on the eve of an electoral process that was considerably discredited because of the way it was set up, saw a combination of power factors within the armed forces. There was the resentment of a group of generals retired by Montesinos and Fujimori and a rift between officers of the artillery and those of the infantry and cavalry, traditionally the most powerful in the army. This had created a movement against the presidential adviser and the armed forces commander in chief, among other officers. But it was not, as the official government communiqué put it, an attempt to murder the de facto president. It was a settling of accounts on the part of the government against certain officers who were secretly discussing a return to constitutional life after 5 April 1992. These officers had also organized a movement with civilian links aimed at putting Máximo San Román in the presidency. Months before San Román had been appointed by the dissolved Congress to substitute Fujimori, who had put himself outside of the law by heading the 5 April coup. The kind of coup attempt circulated by the government was simply absurd. It had been attributed to a group of retired officers, in complicity with a handful of mid-echelon men on active duty with no troops under them and no barracks on their side, who supposedly were trying to kill Fujimori. As the accused parties pointed out, a coup d'état is not made with retired military men and without troops.

The real coup attempt that had been in the making was of much greater dimensions and was diligently aborted by the intelligence service of the regime. Besides, several of the accused mentioned in the official Fujimori communiqué, who were signaled as being under arrest, such as General José Pastor, turned up the next day (Saturday, 14 November) completely free and relaxing at home where they had been all day as well as the previous night. So the speculation then was of some ill feeling within a sector of the army against a hoax engineered by the government, which refused to arrest the coup makers. The day after the coup attempt the unofficial government paper, *Expreso*, pointed to General Valdivia, who had played such an important role in the Fujimori coup, as being behind the countercoup. However, this man, the army chief of staff, who was not named in the official communiqué as being responsible for anything, was free and carrying out his duties; only two days later he was put under a sort of house arrest, and then almost immediately released and restored to his position. There was something grotesque about a man being accused of trying to kill the de facto president and the army commander in chief, and being put under house arrest only two days after the events, during which time he certainly could have fled or gone into hiding. In addition, nothing was said of other active-duty officers who supposedly participated in the coup attempt.

A coup maker out to assassinate the president does not wait for them to come and arrest him at home. And loyal military men responsible for arresting coup makers do not wait two days to do so, unless they are waiting to comply with orders worked out by Montesinos and Fujimori. This offers some idea of the strong rivalries within the army itself. Or perhaps it had taken two days for these military men to find out about a coup d'état that they themselves had just blocked. The grotesque aspect of it all was emphasized when no foreign government issued a single communiqué of solidarity with the Peruvian government, obviously showing that they just could not believe what had happened. In any case, some officers were put in jail. General Jaime Salinas, who had strongly opposed Fujimori's coup, was the most prominent military man sent to prison after the events. His high reputation within the military and his constitutionalist position in justifying his move against Fujimori must have been a decisive factor in the de facto government's strike against him. Several generals spoke in favor of Salinas's release after the event, in what was strong evidence of rifts within the military. General Arciniega, in particular, was forced to seek asylum at the Argentinian embassy following threats that he attributed to Montesinos. That episode was not the only evidence of cracks within the military structure. In early May 1993, division General Rodolfo Robles Espinoza of the Peruvian army took refuge in the American embassy in Lima after revealing, in a public communication, that Vladimiro Montesinos and Bari Hermoza had ordered Major Martín Rivas to organize a "death squad." According to General Robles, until then chief of the instruction and doctrine command of the army and widely regarded as the third man in the military hierarchy, this "death squad" was responsible for the disappearence of nine students and one professor from the university of *La Cantuta* and for the death of ten people in Barrios Altos, Lima, in November 1992.

Today's Peruvian politics, then, is carried out in the barracks, amid the power struggle among different forces within the military apparatus. Men like Montesinos and the head of the army wield power, control what needs to be controlled, and invent such operations as the above in order to affirm their power in the face of potentially rebellious military men. When their rivals gather enough strength to get rid of them, they will move in to govern. It is impossible to tell whether their self-professed loyalty to the Constitution, which was canceled by Fujimori, will prove sincere in such event. Since 5 April 1992 the legitimacy of the Constitution has been replaced by the legitimacy of force. This is a sort of quicksand where nothing permanent is guaranteed. Everything depends on the person who at any given moment seems to have the greatest strength. The permanence of Fujimori depends on this correlation of forces within the military apparatus. The situation in today's Peru is clearly expressed in a statement that used to be made about the old medieval Hapsburg rule: "Despotism moderated by confusion" ("*Despotismus gemildert durch Schlamperi*").[5]

Notes

1. *Cholo* is the Peruvian word used to describe the dark-faced *mestizo*, and *chino* means "chinaman," a word used in reference to the Asian origin of Señor Fujimori, who is in fact Japanese.
2. That is to say, in the European sense of defenders of freedom in all its forms. This will be the sense in which the word "liberal" will be used throughout the book.
3. José González, "Guerrillas and Coca in the Upper Huallaga Valley," in *Shining Path of Peru*, edited by David Scott Palmer (New York: St. Martin's Press, 1992).
4. Rogelio García Lupo, "Narcos peruanos delataron al líder de Sendero Luminoso" ("Peruvian Drug Dealers Turned in the Leader of *Sendero Luminoso*"), *Tiempo* (Madrid), (5 October 1992).
5. Jean-Francois Revel, *Le regain démocratique* (Paris: Fayard, 1992).

2

The *Caudillos* and the Adam Complex

All despotic regimes, be they benevolent or belligerent, ruling in Latin America from the time of emancipation around the beginning of the last century have sought sources of legitimacy. The only exception to the rule is perhaps the first wave of military or civilian *caudillos* (almost always military) who managed to stay in power for some time. The early Latin American political leaders came directly from the independence struggle. This was an essentially military effort led by *criollos*,[1] Latin Americans of Spanish descent who were brought together by certain liberal and modern ideas. From the first day they saw in their task the marriage of arms and reason, force and ideas. This political-military alliance hanging from the rifles of the patriots very quickly invaded the first political efforts in the independent republics and made for a period of military rulers. In Peru, for example, owing to circumstances and an undefined war, San Martín, the liberator of Lima, became the "Protector" of the independent nation; and in 1823 the first president was General José de la Riva Agüero.

This initial stage of Latin American republics wavered between the anarchy of passing visionary bosses, some more consistent than others, and a different form of *caudillo* who would be lasting and stable and able to leave his impression on the history of the continent. That first generation of stable *caudillos* is perhaps the only one in a long tradition that weaves, like Ariadne's thread, through our republican labyrinth, that was not obsessed with the idea of legitimacy. All of them, in one way or another, tried to convince themselves and their subjects that their republics must be ruled by them. But no political program accompanied this affirmation, nor did it rest on a rationalization based on gluing the power of force to formulas of legitimacy generally accepted among the people being governed.

Belonging to this generation of dictators with no desire for legitimacy was the well-known José Gaspar Rodríguez Francia, the same Doctor Francia who fascinated Carlyle. He ruled for thirty-five years in Paraguay until his death in 1840. We also have the Mexican general Santa Anna who headed his country's government off and on during the 1830s, 1840s, and 1850s. He has come to make up part of the historical menagerie thanks to the fact that in a Mexico City cemetery, among throngs of supporters, he buried the leg he had lost fighting against French troops. Then there is Manuel Rosas from Argentina. He ruled in the first half of the nineteenth century from the province of Buenos Aires with an iron hand and a centralist focus after having been a provincial *caudillo* and a mortal enemy of the *unitarios*, the centralist forces from the capital.

This generation of lasting dictators belongs to a rather rural era in republican life. The men were backed by landowners and the bayonets of the military, and they were constricted by the *criollo* atmosphere in which political battles developed. Meanwhile the rest of the nation carried on its normal life, that is, the same life it lived immediately before independence and that had quietly slipped into the republic, due to the absence of reforms. These *caudillos* killed, jailed, and fornicated; but they made no reforms and did not pretend to create a legal framework for their activities. There is only one *caudillo* from this generation who broke with the norm: Latorre in Uruguay. He said, "these people are ungovernable," and he left.

After that first generation of long-lived dictators, things changed and there followed different generations of Latin American dictators acting on ideas, rudimentary or sophisticated, which, feeding on the social and political decomposition of the countries in question and the weakness of ignorance faced with promises and demagogy, tried to endow their own power, both externally and internally, with some authority. These men tried with greater or lesser emphasis and with greater or lesser luck (normally without any) to leave a mark on their time through reforms, public works, or statements of intent emerging from made-to-order constitutions. For example, the well-known Peruvian political *caudillo*, Ramón Castilla, pushed through three constitutions and a statute in the middle of the last century.

Latin American dictatorships took on, after that first exceptional generation, characteristics that are still seen today and have become more or less traditional. Although it should be pointed out that within the dictatorial tradition there have been very different models, varied sources of legitimacy, and ideological approaches often at odds with one another. In the second half of the past century, with the business and industrial world becoming part of the dictatorial political complex, Latin American dictatorship acquired truly national dimensions. And it began a search for a justification and an ethic under which the blend of interests that composed it could be wrapped. With the exception of José Batlle y Ordoñez in Uruguay who brought in the most surprising democratic reforms on the continent (although he contributed decisively to the welfare state that would in time prove such a wreck), the *caudillos* discovered that it was possible to be a despot and call oneself a democrat, to be a murderer and profess the value of goodness, to know oneself a dictator and believe oneself legal, to rule like a tyrant and sign a constitution.

Juridical positivism hit the Latin American continent like a maelstrom, and it convinced rulers that one could change the world through the simple approval of laws and norms. It also showed that legality emanates from the man who governs, rather than the opposite, and that the creation of legality from a position of power can bring in an era that, as well as being legitimate, will operate on real-life transformations carefully outlined on paper. This notion leaves very little in the hands of chance or the imponderable. It means governing, from a position of power, the conduct of the individual and foreseeing the result according to lthe instrument of the law. This political philosophy, which took root on the continent in the nineteenth century and spread through the republics, became feverishly popular in this century and infiltrated the policies of the various governments, dictatorial or democratic, military or civilian. But regarding what concerns us here, it is sufficient to stress its influence on the creation of this new type of dictator that followed the first wave of *caudillos* and continues today.

Without understanding this historical characteristic, it will be impossible to understand and discuss in today's Peru the dictatorship of Alberto Fujimori. His obsession with constructing a theoretical basis and a legitimacy is heir to this long Latin American tradition. The dictatorship responded to international pressure favoring democratization with improvisation and a constantly changing political calendar. This leads to the conclusion that Fujimori's project lacks both ideological foundations and a sense of confidence in his own form of understanding legitimacy. Besides, the intellectual poverty of his government's management makes it obvious that we have, from a theoretical point of view, one of the least sophisticated dictatorships in the history of Peru. But this is not very important. What does matter is that in the wake of the confusion we saw, from the first moment, a political discourse full of reasons and justifications in its desperate search for legitimacy. It is not a merely circumstantial discourse out to present the coup as a situational response to an ephemeral political crisis. It is a government project whose goal is to endure and grow. It is even aimed at other Latin American countries and it offers each of its acts a legal framework from which its authority can emerge. It is a poor and disjointed approach, but unmistakable in nature: it wants to lay a border between something embedded in the past, which we could call the old regime, and a new era, a new form of government, a new form of state-society relations that will supplant democracy as democrats understand it. Proof that this is the line of thought of the regime is that, just like all the other Latin American dictators out to legitimize themselves via something more than simply governing, Fujimori claims he is a democrat and that his actions will tend to bring about "real democracy." This is the distinct sign of someone in search of legitimacy.

We face, therefore, once again in Latin American history, an "Adam complex." Democracy is born for the first time: this is, at last, real democracy. Its pioneering character allows it to survive comparisons with the dictatorial Latin American past. Faced with the terrible state of affairs of today and yesterday, the promise of a redeeming future has a legitimizing impact on the people. By conferring on the dictatorship the characteristics of founder of, and starting point for, real democracy, the ruler divests democrats of their main argument: that democracy existed already, that what had to be done was exploit its possibilities and enrich its content. And since everything that came before was not authentic democracy, the legitimization of the dictatorship begins with a negative act: the elimination of the past as a theoretical reference to the current situation. After that, we have the constructive phase, the articulation, although improvised, of a positivist discourse founded upon the realities emanating from the new regime, which begin to emanate due to the destruction of an undesirable past. All necessary authority is there, with no reference to any previous legal or theoretical framework.

This pattern is ancient history in our countries. One *caudillo* after another has tried to justify himself. In the first half of this century, for example, we saw the thriving of *caudillos* obsessed with public investment: Pérez Jiménez in Venezuela, Trujillo in the Dominican Republic, and Odría in Peru. The first talked about "sowing petroleum" so that the richness of the land might bear fruits. Odría demanded "works and not words." From an anticommunist position they all believed the state was a source of social well-being. A different generation of socialist or socializing *caudillos* shared, from an opposite side of the ideological spectrum, the conception of economic and social life as a "strategic area." As such they were part of the scope of the state, of the national government. Those men were Getulio Vargas in Brazil, Perón in Argentina, Paz Estenssoro in Bolivia, Arbenz in Guatemala, Torrijos in Panama, Velasco in Peru, Castro in Cuba, and Allende in Chile. The decade of the 1970s saw, with right-wing military men like Videla in Argentina or left-wing rulers like Velasco in Peru, the prolongation of this line of Latin American *caudillos*. Ideological differences aside, they offer a space and time unity for the phenomenon of Latin American state and government and shape the system that our generation inherits.

The sources of legitimacy can always be found within the juridical formulas that these rulers create. In almost all the cases in question, the ruler—the *caudillo*—establishes a border between his rule and what came before him. This is at once a break and a beginning. The case of Alberto Fujimori became at once part of this Latin American tradition. His approach as of 5 April became a condemnation of a past without real democracy. Here he included all forms of government Peru had ever had, and announced an authentic democracy once and for all. Among the various statements advisers have given Fujimori to mouth in order to offer the dictatorship legitimacy there is little said of the fact that this *caudillo* was chosen in fair elections in 1990. There is, rather, a reasoning that goes beyond electoral contingencies and constitutes an atemporal truth not subject to an electoral schedule. But of course he still offered a multitude of contradictory calendars to appease the international response with promises of a return to democracy. Fujimori insists strongly that real democracy in Peru came to life on 5 April 1992, and that the new Peruvian republic was born on that date (*Sendero Luminoso* also speaks of a "new republic").

So we see Fujimori placing himself within the old tradition of the Latin American *caudillos* who, depending on the ignorance of broad sectors of the population concerning the political history of their nations, tried to dodge the links between their dictatorships and efforts to legitimize them, and the sort of antidemocratic *caudillos* coming earlier who also worked out political-juridical systems as alibis for their acts. In the case of Fujimori this is especially striking, because in Peru there have been a multitude of bosses who in their time claimed to embody real democracies. They assaulted Congress and saw to the election of new membes, and they would manipulate the elections.

From José de la Riva Agüero, the first president of the republic in 1823, to Alberto Fujimori, Peru has only sporadically seen periods of democracy bringing together an honestly elected president, a Parliament emerging from free elections, and a system of checks and balances where the will of the man governing was not above the law but subject to it. Riva Agüero inaugurated an era of Peruvian presidents in the first quarter of the last century with an act of force. In the midst of war, in 1823, there was the "Balconcillo mutiny." Lima troops demanded the naming of Riva Agüero and an end to the junta who had been governing. Shortly after, Simón Bolívar, who had finished the independence struggle in Peru begun by San Martín from Argentina, proclaimed himself dictator within the framework of a Constitution that made him president for life. A victim of his own ethics, he was removed from power by force in 1827.

Since that time and along the lines of this first stage there have been *caudillos*, civilian and military, tall and short, ugly and handsome, white and mestizo, well-spoken and illiterate, and cool-headed and angry. Sometimes, as in the case of Luis Sánchez Cerro in 1930, they led a coup d'état against a dictator. In other cases, like Velasco in 1968, they overthrew a democratic ruler. Still other times (as in the case of Sánchez Cerro in 1931) they won legitimate elections followed by a persecution of opposition parliamentarians and the destruction of a Congress that had been elected along with the government. Then we have Odría in 1950. He called elections after ruling for some time with no Parliament and no elections. It was a sinister and manipulated process that finally produced servile legislators and a self-proclaimed legitimacy. In 1919 Augusto Leguía began a dictatorship that lasted eleven years. It was not hard for him to do away with the legislative power, although that institution had worked democratically since 1895, set up a new one, and invent a Constitution made to measure. There was also Guillermo Billinghurst. In 1914 this *caudillo* also did away with legislative power. But he was not able to prevent the military establishment from doing him in, thanks to the weakness of juridical and political power. Another example is General Benavides. In 1936 he saw that a candidate backed by the opposition would be elected. So he convinced the Congress to extend his term for three years. This brought about the peculiar situation of a coup d'état carried out by Congress itself. The case of Alberto Fujimori is exactly the opposite from that of Benavides.

The above is only a handful of examples of different Peruvian dictators, before Alberto Fujimori, who, throughout our republican history, have created a pretense of democracy in order to carry the country along a route of progress. Each in his own way used previously established democratic ins and outs or invented democratic subterfuges offering his cause legitimacy in the face of time, the country, and history. Peru is not alone among Latin American countries, a majority of them, in which the dictator-*caudillo*, civilian or military, leftist or rightist, has hindered the creation of lasting democratic institutions, a decent ethic governing state-society relationships, the links between the individual and power, and the birth of an institutional hierarchy that might put force at the service of the rule of law and not the opposite.

Among the many *caudillos* in each country there is always one who stands out because his name becomes a symbol of the rest. In Brazil the example is Getulio Vargas, born in Río Grande do Sul and Liberal Alliance presidential candidate in 1930. He was defeated at the ballot box but came to power on the crest of a revolution claiming electoral fraud. In 1937, along the lines of the *caudillo* system, he proclaimed a "New State" that concentrated power in his own hands. He persecuted the opposition and remained in office until 1945. He was not a particularly bloody dictator. He promoted the industrialization of the nation and brought in such reforms as the labor code of 1943.

In Argentina the man's name is Hipólito Irigoyen. He was the Radical party candidate who won in the 1926 elections, becoming the first president representing that party. He was much less shameless than Vargas as a *caudillo*, and he gave up power at the end of his first term. But his government, while it did bring in certain social reforms, was autocratic and crushed the autonomy of the provinces and Congress itself. In Bolivia there was Víctor Paz Estenssoro. He led the National Revolutionary Movement and came to power in 1952 when a socialist revolution brought down the military junta. He also brought in an era of social reforms and, just like all the other *caudillos*, pulled the democratic strings to rule in an antidemocratic fashion and invented a Constitution to suit him. In Paraguay it was General Alfredo Stroessner who took power originally in 1955. From 1959 to 1989 he got himself elected and re-elected eight times thanks to a Constitution designed to give him an aura of legality. And legislative eagerness did not abandon the Brazilian dictatorship of the 1970s either: from 1969 to 1974 there was a purely cosmetic Congress forming part of its court.

This is only a handful of the myriad *caudillos* and dictators in the history of the Americas. We see that the differences among them are less important than what they had in common. They all stubbornly contributed to a frustration of Latin American democracy through a combination of democratic tricks and brutal acts of force, which, in the aura of a concocted legitimacy and ambitious projects for social reform, are responsible for the barbarity and backwardness that stretches from the Río Grande to the Strait of Magellan.

So when Fujimori presents his plans as a break with the Peruvian past he is falsifying the real nature of his regime. He is doing the same as almost all the Latin American *caudillos* who claimed they were founding a new way of approaching society-government relations. The fact that Fujimori is a civilian and not from the military does not separate him from the tradition of *caudillos* and dictators on the continent. As we have seen, a good part of those who came before him were civilians who under various circumstances took advantage of regimes that had allowed them to take power. In some cases (Vargas and Leguía) they burst forth against what they felt was an attempt to rob them of a legitimate victory. The case of Paz Estenssoro is that of a man heading a revolution against a despotic government. In other cases—very similar to that of Fujimori—it was a question of winning clean elections with no problems in taking power; but once in control they betrayed democracy.

Among this latter list of dictators one finds those, like Juan María Bordaberry in Uruguay in the first half of the 1970s, who were nothing but civilian puppets for a military takeover. There were others like Mariano Ospina Pérez in Colombia who in the second half of the 1940s personally led the forces of law and order in the transformation of the government to a dictatorship via the closing down of a democratic Congress and assaults on the opposition. The fact that, in accordance with the electoral calendar, Ospina Pérez handed over power to Laureano Gómez (the only candidate) in 1950 does not make the former a democrat. In the same way, Perón won the 1946 elections in Argentina and three years later invented a Constitution to keep him in power and systematically weakened democratic institutions.

The fact that Fujimori was elected fairly does not separate him from the tradition of Latin American despotism. We have seen that the list of *caudillos* coming to power democratically and then ripping the system apart is as long as that of the military dictators. And there are no attenuating factors in the fact that one might come to dictatorial power with less violence than that which one associates with a traditional dictatorship. There was sufficient violence in Peru used during the first days; and the subsequent "normalization" is directly proportional to the passivity of the population, the giving in of the media, and the inability of certain political parties, naturally very discredited, to mobilize public opinion.

Something similar happened in 1952 in Cuba. The people responded with absolute indifference to the Batista coup. So it was not necessary to use much violence at the beginning of his dictatorship. No one died on the day of the coup and, as we all know, the dictator himself pardoned Fidel Castro after his important attack on the Moncada Barracks. This allowed the latter to travel abroad and organize resistance. Pinochet, on the other hand, had to use violence in Chile from day one in 1973. He was faced with a powerful Marxist opposition, which was in the minority but was not ready to accept power in the hands of the military.

In all cases there is a link among the Latin American dictatorial figures: a break with the past. The past is morally corrupt, politically despotic, and socially fragmenting, whether there governs an oligarchy or a *soi disant* protelarian clique as an enemy of the oligarchy. There must be a new republic that is morally decent, politically democratic, and socially just.

A factor that has not always been present and that cannot be pointed to as essential regarding the Latin American dictator-*caudillo* is anti-imperialism. But in the majority of cases there was always a vaguely nationalist factor that went from the revindication of a glorious past

(Velasco spoke of a "socialist era" among the Incas in Peru) to a denouncing of foreign intervention (Pinochet lashed out at Soviet-Cuban intervention in Allende's Chile and the Sandinistas hit hard against Somoza as a pro-U.S. *vendepatrias* in Nicaragua). Fujimori is among the *caudillos* for whom this nationalist factor is circumstantial rather than essential: it is merely useful in canceling out the resistance to his coup as "a betrayal of the fatherland." The remaining factors common to Latin American dictatorship, however, are present in the regime that was installed in Peru on 5 April 1992 and could already be detected in the 1990-92 democratic period of the Fujimori presidency. They link the Peruvian regime to the antidemocratic historical tradition of Latin America.

One main agrument of the Peruvian coup makers—an idea that is prevalent in Latin America today—has been that the traditional political parties are wasted. Their antidemocratic and corrupt practices have blocked the development of real democracy, and they have lost the confidence of the people. They are in no condition to offer the system the moral and political force necessary for the creation of respectable institutions. This is a central theme of today's Peruvian republic, and of most Latin American republics, which the government has conveniently used to justify its plans.

There is nothing new here. A good part of the Latin American coups on the right and on the left have been against "corrupt politicians." And the essential argument of the dictatorial adventures has always been that paternalistic line that considers the leadership of the nation something too serious to be left in the hands of politicians. The Peru of the 1990s offers more antipolitician arguments than ever before. There is a state of mind hostile to what is even indirectly associated with traditional politics. And such a state of mind is not unfounded. In effect, one of the great frustrations of the Peruvian republic is the absence of a dynamic, modern, and transparent democracy of parties. It is a tragedy for Peru that this reality has led to the conclusion that an authoritarian system of power propped up by military force is the solution to such a state of affairs, because it reveals a confusion with regard to the root of the evil. In the first place, one forgets that Peru's most traditional political party, the one that has governed longest and has most directly influenced the evolution (the involution, really) of our institutional life is the Peruvian army. People also forget that the essence of the problem does not lie in the democratic system that has existed in Peru only sporadically, but in the absence of a sustained democracy within which political life might have developed differently. It has not been democracy, but the lack of it, that has brought Peru to its current state. It has not been the political party system, but the absence of a permanent institutional life with political parties linked to an ongoing democracy, that has brought on this total failure of civilian politics from which Peruvians, and other Latin Americans, of the 1990s are despairing.

The Peruvian republic lay down the guidelines from the beginning, strengthening military options in the development of political life. The republic of Peru was born under the sign of instability. This can be seen in the very origin of its independence. The first Constitution is in fact the one promulgated in 1812 in Cádiz, Spain, while Peru was still a colony. Spanish liberals, faced with the advance of the Napoleonic invaders and taking advantage of the defeat of Fernando VII, modernized the legal regime and did away with absolutism. These events were a sort of detonator for independence movements in Latin America. And they also created for the future a strong focus of tension in the newly independent republics, for two reasons. First, because the viceroys in the Latin American colonies did not completely respect the new Constitution also in effect in the Americas (several delegates from Latin America had attended the *Cortes de Cádiz*). In failing to do so, they did away with their very legitimacy and established what would be in the future a permanent republican incapacity to establish systems ruled by law and not by will. In addition, the king himself re-established absolutism in 1814, recognized once again the liberal Constitution in 1820, only to bring down the *Cortes* and return once more to an absolutist regime in 1823. In doing so he established a precedent for constitutional and legal instability in the colonies. In 1816 the Spanish troops smashed the first pro-independence forces in the Americas. By then, in addition to the natural anticolonial rejection on the part of *criollos* from the colonies, the conditions were there for the obsession with legitimacy to get enmeshed with the fighting. So arms and the law were born in a tangle, the latter losing out to the former.

In this way, the Peruvian republic came to endure a half-century of military governments. It was only in 1872, with the election of Manuel Pardo, leader of the Civilian party, that nonmilitary men took over the presidency. In the previous period civilians played roles that historian

Jorge Basadre has called that of *validos* and *censores* ("courtiers" and "censors").[2] That is, they were mere instruments or parasites with respect to military power. Their job was to put arguments into the mouths of the bosses who, in Lima or Arequipa, would rise up against the government and do away with it. Once power was grabbed, they would play minor roles.

Moved by the stagnation of an economic system scarcely apt for the creation of wealth, lawyers and priests sought out public posts. In time, this became a tradition. Civilian participation in the affairs of the state became mere bureaucracy: the invention and perpetuation of public posts. The most outstanding creation of this stage in our republic is the army. It was at once the child and father of independence and, as such, the vector of the legitimacy born with it. The army became the only road to social integration in Peru. Several of the *caudillos* were mestizos. The rest of the institutions accentuated the vast social gaps inherited from the conquest. The result, on the coast as well as the sierra, was a static system, an order with little mobility or permeability.

This is not to say that there were no currents of political thought. On the contrary, there were very rich ones. One of the republican misfortunes of Peru is that these did not coalesce in stable and lasting civilian political organizations; nor could they run the government of Peru. Subject to the military reality and the whims of the *caudillos*, civilians were almost without exception incapable of putting across their ideas consistently.

Peru had seven constitutions between 1823 and 1867. The majority were liberal, and a couple of them rather conservative. Not one could stay afloat and become the basis for institutional life. The Constitution was not above contingencies, it was the image of them. Even such rulers as Ramón Castilla in the mid-nineteenth century, who brought in liberal reforms like an end to tribute and slavery, could place his reforms at the service of militarism and authoritarianism, blocking the creation of solid civilian institutions.

It is unfortunate that the Progressive Club in those years amounted to no more than a liberal pressure group; or that the Colegio Guadalupe was more or less the same; or that the progressive Constitution of 1856 was not defended by the country when the soldiers smashed it; or that men like José Gálvez were unable to found a lasting political organization and were content with only a slight influence on the state of affairs in the form of a short-lived ministry; or that Manuel Vidaurre earlier got no response to his proposal to establish modern legal codes based on liberalism to replace those inherited from colonialism.

Peruvian liberals had turned the country into a republic instead of a monarchy, but this early triumph was not consolidated in the decades to follow. And neither were the conservatives able to establish a civilian political force. Names like that of Bartolomé Herrera were lost in the tumult of the times. The conservatives never managed to govern as such. They were content to stand on the sidelines of power and enliven the system the country had inherited from the previous period, and which the military *caudillo* era had made even worse.

The birth of the Civilian party in the final third of the past century seemed to provide new hope for the republic, but frustration was not long in coming. The party came to life within a system that the republic had been strengthening for several decades. It was a movement that expressed the reality of social and economic power, not a force for modernization and change. To a certain extent, this is understandable: with the frustration of lasting civilian institutions and movements, the republic—which had gone on developing a mercantilist, rentier, and plutocratic system— engendered a first civilian political force made in the image of those same vices being hatched by political tradition. The Civilian party was made up of an economic elite, rather than a family-based aristocracy. It was an élite formed around the *guano* business, which dominated Peruvian economy on the basis of consignment, a mercantilist system *par excellence* granting a private monopoly safeguarded by the state.[3] When the state took away the consignments from Peruvian monopolists and gave them over to foreign capital, local people reacted. Other interests, for example, those of *hacienda* owners (that is, landowerns), became involved in the civilian movement. The civilian movement expressed the interests of a class that was tiny in number but very powerful and socially divorced from the great majority of Peruvians who were not the owners of wealth. The system had not promoted a middle class, and it scarcely existed. The presence of people from the interior was small.

Civilian politics, then, emerged from this social strata as a product of economic interests. This party lasted some fifty years, and held power several times between 1872 and 1915. Although its orientation was liberal, its essence was, like the system it embodied, an enemy of participation. It transferred the evils of the economy and the society to Peruvian politics. It was a civilian reaction coming too late in the face of reality, to a large extent because of political impediments that militarism had forced on the civilians from the beginning. For the first time in Peru's history, and so far also the last, it was a genuine effort to get away from the *caudillo* temptation and to constantly renew its leadership. However, even its merits were lost in the failures of its time. Had the civilian movement been born fifty years earlier, perhaps by 1872 we would have seen a different, truly liberal thrust in Peruvian politics. It would not only have based itself on principles like the separation of church and state; it would have had an authentically participatory concept of political power, seeking to bring into its project something more than a little group of monopolists and investors from the national economy and to fix itself firmly in a conception of modern capitalism.

Another republican frustration in Peru is the absence of a bipartisan system. It could have emerged at the end of the last century when another grouping, the Democratic party, appeared under the leadership of Nicolás de Piérola after the war against Chile. This party was also guilty of such national vices as the *caudillo* system and populism. Its ideology was conservative, and in theory it tended to place itself on the opposite side of the Civilian party. But it had the virture of incorporating the masses, for the first time, into Peruvian politics. That was, of course, a double-edged sword. There emerged, together with massive participation in Peruvian politics, political populism. The civilian movement, which initially cooperated with the Democratic party, later closed the doors of power to their old partners in the tradition of antidemocratic practices. Two evils, therefore, the *caudillo* lineage and an absence of democracy, frustrated the existence of this party. The first one is the responsibility of Piérola; the second, that of his enemies.

So civilians in Peru were, as of the end of the last century, as responsible as the military men for the frustration of a democratic project that might have brought about periodic changes in power. In such a climate the parties themselves blocked one another. There were no institutional channels allowing them to live apart from power. Inevitably, the Democratic party, with the doors of power closed to it, died away, unable to survive its leader.

Peru's other great wave of civilian political action came in the 1930s with the Revolutionary Union (UR) and the APRA party. The first was another *caudillo*-oriented grouping. Although it survived the leadership of Sánchez Cerro, the blocking of elections in 1936 and 1939 (typical in our history) made it impossible for the party to carry on within the democratic system.

The APRA, on the other hand, was a response—first on the part of students, and later on the part of an emerging middle class—to Peru's social conditions since independence. It was socialist, but its leader, Haya de la Torre, distanced himself from European Marxist totalitarianism. In this case as well, the absence of democracy in the country had a decisive influence on the party. The party was declared illegal until 1945, and its leader was persecuted. It was only in 1956 that APRA finally became legal. Later, in 1962, its victory at the polls was killed by a new coup d'état.

Amid the civil war climate of the 1930s there emerged a new evil in Peruvian politics: the anti-APRA movement. Civil strife took the lives of many and pushed the UR as well as APRA toward fascist tendencies. Both groupings, which might have successfully constituted the two-party formula that had fallen apart with the Civilian party and the Democratic party, were victims of the absence of democracy and were equally responsible, because of the violence they practiced, for the fact that democracy did not emerge. This goes a long way toward explaining the fact that when APRA came to power in 1985 with Alan García it had not modernized its political ideas and practices and maintained the old nationalist, statist, and authoritarian schemes of its beginnings. The absence of democracy in Peru froze one of its historical parties in time. The other, the UR, died.

The next group of political parties appeared in the second half of the 1950s with *Acción Popular* (Popular Action party) and the Christian Democrats. The latter eventually became the Popular Christian party. The first is a middle-class party that filled the gap left by APRA's former competitors. It thrived against the Odría dictatorship and attempted to be a democratic response to the intolerant tradition in Peruvian politics. It also came down on the side of social reform against the still, paralyzing social order of the nation. But it suffered from two evils: the *caudillo* tradition, once again, and the absence of ideological thought and a clear vision of society-state relations. The Christian Democrats, on the other hand, did have a vision. They took on the social doctrine of the church and attempted to become a bridge between socialism and liberalism. But they emerged rather as a club of outstanding citizens, a group of professionals with no popular support and no capacity to mobilize the country.

Their failure also indicates a vice of Peruvian politics. In a world where political power has almost always operated apart from ideas, doctrines, and ideologies, the political party that did have an overall vision of what society should be lacked, and still lacks, the flair of popular politics.

These parties emerging in recent times are middle-class. The middle class has grown over the decades, becoming a more significant part of society than it was in the past century and the beginning of this one; however, it is still relatively small and far from prosperous, which perpetuates the problem suffered by previous parties: the fact that they cannot represent the nation as a whole. In the provinces the parties depend on *caciquismo*, the local boss system, which is the antithesis of participation. It does give the interior a nexus with the politics of the capital, which the first Peruvian political organizations lacked, but it rests on small local power groups. Economically and socially less important than leaders in Lima, these groups impede mobility and change in any party and understand political activity as a source of income (legal or illegal), rather than an instrument of action favoring certain ideas. Because of its static nature, we can speak of a political cast. Its vices are the expression of a reality, the absence of democracy, the origins of which are entwined in the history of the republic.

These are not all the political parties Peru has seen. There have been many more. But they were short-lived and generally created to serve the political structure of a ruler who was already in power or of one who wanted to use them to get power. These are the main ones, apart from the the Marxist left, which constitutes a special case. The Marxist left had a very strong showing in the Constituent Assembly elections of 1978, and by 1983 it had won the mayoralty of Lima. With a third of all votes, it became the most powerful Marxist electoral force in the Americas. But it succumbed to the illness of all Marxist currents: factionalist tendencies. So while the United Left coalition did become powerful, at the end of the 1980s it became divided again and, struck by communism's universal crisis, began to fade.

Just like the APRA, this left has its roots around the end of the 1920s, when José Carlos Mariátegui founded the Socialist party. From that time on it lived in the shadow of APRA which robbed it of much of its political clientele. It suffered as well the frustrations of illegality due to authoritarian governments. In 1985 with the semisocialist government of Alan García, this left underwent a new and devastating identity crisis.

Presently, its only legacy is the General Workers Union (Central General de Trabajadores), a powerful trade union movement. However, in a country where scarcely 11 percent of the workers are unionized and the vast quantity are working illegally, its strength is only relative.

Instability, militarism, the *caudillo* tradition, and mercantilism, which controlled the Peruvian republic for several decades permeated civilian organizations at their birth and shaped them for the future. Liberal thought was a fleeting shadow in the republican panorama and never organized itself politically. It could be found here and there adorning the speeches of parties, which in their essence were the negation of liberalism. So the only option that might emerge in opposition to the status quo was on the left. It had two currents: APRA and communism. Liberalism was mistaken for a system that had been in fact its total negation. But neither was socialism allowed to develop along institutional channels. Its turbulent and semiclandestine existence froze it in a vision pertaining to the beginnings of the century, which it had imported from the Europe of those years, and it was radicalized and militarized. In many cases this frustration led these parties into alliances with the very system they were struggling against. APRA came to an agreement with authoritarian President Manuel Prado and helped bring down democracy during the first democratic government of Belaunde. The Communist party collaborated with the Velasco military dictatorship. Among the main contemporary parties only the Popular Action party (led by Belaunde) and the Popular Christian party are blameless regarding democratic conduct. However, during the 1980-85 government, where the second was allied with the first in power, the necessary Peruvian state reform was not carried out. There was a perpetuation of state control and socialist tendencies inherited from the past, despite their very different approach to Peru's sufferings. So they contributed to Peru's impoverishment and indirectly to a frustration of the country's democracy.

During the 1990 electoral campaign the Democratic Front made the defense of a party democracy one of the "hobbyhorses" of its discourse. Time and time again the *Sawyer and Miller* advisers and our own people recommended that we break with those "rightist" parties, because the country was crying out for an option apart from the traditional political movements. Our consistent argument was that it would be a great error to blame the political parties per se for the vices of the political system in Peru within which they had developed. It was not democracy that had failed, but something different: the absence of democracy throughout our history. And when democracy did exist, there had been the absence of a great liberal capitalist reform aimed at creating a vast and dynamic market economy within which, without state interference, there could be an integration of the different Perus that had lived with difficulty and often violently from remote times. In order to modernize the parties we had them subscribe to a government plan presented to the country in a completely open fashion (even at times with excessive transparency). They were never in full agreement, but they had to accept since the electors seemed to be on the side of our independent candidate heading the alliance. As an adversary, Alberto Fujimori was intelligent enough to see that he could use this alliance of traditional parties to discredit us. Coming out against the parties was the best way of getting more votes in Peru at that point.

And it is still the best way today, something made clear by the popular response in favor of the coup d'état and the shady congressional elections of 22 November 1992 where in the absence of Peru's main political parties (APRA, Popular Action party, The *Libertad* Movement, and the Pro-Mariátegui Unified party) the government managed to elect several official lists of congressional members shamelessly backed by the state. So why should the political parties of Peru be more modern, efficient, and upright than the country's other institutions born of, and nourished by, exclusiveness, mercantilism, state control, sinecures, and corruption, which have been endemic to our republican life? Reform of Peruvian parties is one of the many issues still waiting to be solved, part of a broader and general necessity, which means reinforcing civilian institutions and giving them a permanent character. Institutions must be put at the service of a law that is valid for all; they must be made independent of the temporary leadership of individuals and not subject to the political power of the state. Public posts must not continue to be a source of income for thousands of citizens for whom the bureaucracy is a substitute for enterprise and the creation of wealth. To do away with democracy as a system is not a different form of understanding Peruvian life and renewing its political institutions. It is confusing the effect with the cause and following the old path emerging from the last century, sometimes in a zigzag form and sometimes in a straight line.

The Peruvian government of Fujimori, like all dictatorial governments, wants to do away with all political parties. But as a substitution it organizes the same thing: a political party. In the 1920s Augusto Leguía also created his own political structure (which was largely stolen from the Civilian party) to maintain his dictatorship. In the more recent antidemocratic experience with Velasco Alvarado we find ideologist Carlos Delgado creating the National System of Social Mobilization. This functioned as a vast political party, despite the "no-party" thesis maintained by him. Alberto Fujimori has strengthened his original organization, Cambio 90. With former minister Yoshiyama he created a list of politicians for the Constituent Congress elected in November 1992. He also backed a third list headed by politician Rafael Rey and made up of several of Peru's most rancid politicians, among them, Enrique Chinos Soto, a man several times senator and looking for a way to secure a safe position in the power structure. Already during the electoral campaign in 1990 Fujimori showed, as he drew closer to Alan García, a good instinct for using tactics of the old politics, as well as his adaptability to the military structure, which was preparing to take power. The government brandished arguments against politicians; but it developed its own political clientele to function as a bridge between the civilian society and the military power structure. The result was twofold: a terrible confusion in a country that sees the root of all evil in political parties; and, along the lines of the old tradition of political clientele in the country, an opportunistic, bureaucratic, and parasitic excercise of politics bereft of ideas and protected from opposition scrutiny. So while it claimed not to be doing so, the government was really perpetuating an inveterate custom that works for politics as well as economics: to associate success with collusion and complicity with established power. The politicians who back the antipolitical position of Fujimori today are power's parasites. They are what historian Jorge Basadre called their predecessors: *validos* and *censores*.

Popular feelings against politicians and politics were strongly felt during the 1990 electoral campaign. APRA and *Acción Popular* had governed since 1980, and both had failed. APRA had pushed the country from the Third to the Fourth World. It was almost the Africanization of Peru. This disaster played into the hands of a process as old as the history of the republic: a radical rift between citizens and institutions, dragging the majority of the country into an anarchy from which there sometimes emerged imaginitive and legitimate forms of common law. They were not officially legislated, and they did entail a risk for established political order. The country, three-quarters of which was made up of young people, felt that the old structures had rotted. Sooner or later the political world had to suffer on the part of a country that no longer felt tied to the same violent (not necessarily physical) response that other institutional and official entities had undergone. We were aware of this danger during the electoral campaign, and we made an effort to bring together my father's image as an independent and the *Libertad* Movement that he led with the institutional channels embodied in such traditional organizations as the Popular Action party and the Popular Christian party. We brought them into a plan for large-scale state reform and a vast free market integrating the creative forces of that world that had remained in the legal shadows of Peru. An obsession in the campaign was to work for a mandate in the first round of voting. That would allow Parliament to contribute with its absolute majority in both legislative houses to indispensable reforms; and the president, backed by public opinion, would be able to face interest groups that would inevitably try to block change.

One of the most extraordinary paradoxes came precisely in the results of the first round. Almost one-fourth of the voters came out for Fujimori because he was an independent. But electoral arithmetic indicated that the parliamentary bodies, also elected in this first round, would have a majority of politicians who were not independent. Legislators from the independent list representing Cambio 90 did not even make one-fourth of the total. The *Libertad* Movement, which within our alliance was the nontraditional option, did not obtain a preferential vote that might distance it from its own partners. One-fifth of the legislative body was made up of the most traditional party of all, APRA, which was governing the country, due to an incredible vote of around 20 percent. The Peruvian people cast a contradictory vote. They brought an enemy of traditional politics to the presidency in the second round. But they denied that very candidate a majority in the first round and put an overwhelming number of traditional politicians in legislative seats. So Congress was fragmented and perfectly contradictory to the country's state of mind. But that very country had elected such a Congress.

Then, flying in the face of all predictions, Congress began actually to collaborate with Fujimori. It was surely inspired by previous republican experiences when minority governments had been brought down because of their inability to overcome parliamentary adversity and push their political agenda ahead; so, time and time again, the legislators of 1990 showed a spirit of cooperation. For a good part of 1990 and 1991 this frustrated the plans of Fujimori and his advisers, who were out to chase down the parliamentarians systematically and create a confrontation between a renovating government and traditional Peruvian politics. However, the president looked for more and more confrontations. At the beginning of the president's mandate the traditional political parties had given over the leadership of the two legislative houses to Cambio 90, despite the fact that they were in the minority and the men in question had no experience. In addition, taking advantage of a formula used for the first time in 1828, Congress gave the government "extraordinary powers" to rule by decree regarding taxes. Later these powers were broadened to include private investment and the creation of jobs. The legislative bodies finally allowed Fujimori to issue 126 decrees. They modified or threw out only eighteen, in accordance with the Constitution. The 1991 and 1992 budgets were aproved by both houses in collaboration with the minister of the economy. Shortly before the coup, Congress itself rejected a motion of censure against that very minister presented by the opposition. Never in the history of Peru had there been such open collaboration between the legislature and a minority president. This came about precisely because it was felt that it was what the public wanted. A certain guilt complex played its part among traditional politicians whom the people had voted in through the same electoral process that brought Fujimori to power.

There is no validity, then, to the argument that legislative powers had blocked President Fujimori's government from 1990 until the 5 April 1992 coup. Quite the contrary. The ruling party , Cambio 90, a recent creation of Alberto Fujimori, had shown its skill in playing the political game better than the old parties. Lead personally by Fujimori, Cambio 90 voted against legal proceedings of the accused in a parlimentary trial of former president Alan García concerning the Lima prison massacres of 1986. In August 1991, in historical proceedings in the Peruvian Parliament against Alan García for illicit use of funds, Cambio 90 (according to the instructions of Fujimori) voted against the charges, that is, in favor of the exoneration of García, despite the fact it was a parliamentary trial that should have suspended the former president's parliamentary immunity so that the Supreme Court could have the last word.

This was the first time in the history of Peru that a former president had been subject to a parliamentary trial. The case had to do with García's orders to transfer Peruvian reserves in hard currency and gold to the BCCI in Panama during his government (1985-90). The bank was known for its ties with drug dealing, and the interests in question were prejudicial to the country. According to a New York grand jury headed by prosecutor Robert Morganthau, the operations meant commissions paid to high-ranking Peruvian government officials. Besides, there was an imbalance between García's income and expenditures while he was in office. The legislative investigating commission, aided by two private agencies from the United States, had accused García of opening several foreign bank accounts with substantial amounts of dollars. All this was reason enough for legislative proceedings unprecedented in the history of Peru, through which those very traditional politicians, whom public opinion was ac-cusing of corruption, would try to carry the investigation to its ultimate consequences. The prosecution won the final vote. As a result, the immunity of Alan García was suspended. But up to the final moment Alberto Fujimori had tried to block this, offering his party's votes on behalf of the accused. So we should not be surprized to see that the coup opportunely frustrated the investigation regarding charges of corruption against the presidential family made by the nation's first lady. And it is not strange to see that once democratic institutions were smashed cases like that of Transport Minister Alberto Ross were shifted to the back burner. The charges against Mr. Ross came originally from the weekly magazine *Oiga* and were later backed up by other sources. They said he had used his position in the important INTERBANC banking enterprise to acquire dollars coming from drug dealing.

Today it is clear that Fujimori worked at all costs to block the consolidation of a legislative body with moral authority in the face of public opinion. This body, which was brought down by the 5 April 1992 coup (accused of being corrupt, obstructionist, and apathetic to the people, among many other things) despite being made up of so many politicians, was beginning to show signs of being more in tune with public opinion than many others in Peru's history. And the great enemy of traditional politics had shown signs of conduct perfectly in line with the kind of traditional politics the people had angrily rejected. The fact that, further on, the Supreme Court refused to take legal proceedings ordered by the Congress and endorsed by the nation's public prosecutors (another institution that, contrary to tradition, had taken things in hand) does not cast a bit of doubt on the behavior of Parliament, which was one of the main victims of the coup d'état. In any case, if we follow the line of reasoning of the coup makers, the Fujimori government, in backing the accused despite strong evidence that he was guilty, could be considered an accomplice of the Supreme Court, which did nothing but transfer to the judicial level the same conduct that the Cambio 90 government had shown in Parliament. The signal from the Government Palace to the magistrates, in a country where political power has always had a crushing influence on justice, was very clear: Alan García should not be tried.

And so, shaping up in Peru was a political configuration full of echoes from the past: a coup d'état whose principal excuse—a break with a disastrous history and the founding of a new form of understanding power-society relations—was open fraud, a rhetorical subterfuge having no relationship to the essence of things. In the final analysis the history of Peru repeated itself in a slightly new form. The Constituent Congress emerging from the November 1992 elections where Fujimori sought to placate international opinion and give his government some sort of constitutional legitimacy produced a bunch of traditional politicians, some outmoded and some with a younger outlook. But an unmistakable antidemocratic rule brought them together: the fourth complementary disposition. They were forbidden by "law" to annul acts of government. The body had no autonomous budget and its members were forbidden to exercise any parliamentary function for the following ten years. Two weeks before the elections, Fujimori himself declared (*El comercio*, 10 November 1992) that important decisions like the re-election of the president or capital punishment would not be the responsibility of the Constituent Assembly about to be formed, whose only purpose was to write the Constitution of Peru; instead, those decisions would be taken by the "sovereign people" of Peru via referendum. The de facto president was warning that state decisions would not be made by the Constituent Congress but by himself in consultation with the people (this, of course, precludes any notion of the rule of law). One is obliged to ask oneself: even in the case that the Constituent Congress had been elected in a clean electoral process, what is it worth, if the decisions are not to be made by its members ("a little clique of congressmen") but by the chief of state in constant dialogue with the masses, who, furthermore, before the Constituent Congress is even assembled, announces that it will be born dead? This electoral process, like others organized by Latin American dictatorships in the past, was manipulated with state money. The mass media had placed themselves in the service of the government as of the April agression. Magazines were the only source of opposition; but they suffered from a doubling of taxes for imported paper on which they depended. The editor of one of them was sentenced by one of the dictator's judges for calling Montesinos "Rasputin."[4] The armed forces became an authentic "campaign commando." And, according to General Jaime Salinas, they filled in the thousands of names needed for the official list to qualify for the elections, in the face of lacking civilian support. There was an incredible proliferation of official lists (at least three). And legal harassment was endless.

This election was a twin of the one carried off under the Sandinista government of Daniel Ortega in 1984. World public opinion denounced that process as a fraud, despite the fact that some "opponent" or other participated. In Peru, although the main opposition parties of the left, the center, and the right were absent from the elections, and despite the blatant manipulation of the process, the official candidate obtained a little less than 40 percent of the vote, only half the support that the government had been boasting since the 5 April coup. Furthermore, the 20 percent of null and void votes is without precedent in Perú. Never, when traditional politicians dominated the process, had the electorate shown such a rejection of the electoral process.

The vices of Peruvian politics, then, were carried on in the 1990s behind a mask of newness and change. The country, boiling over with impatience, seemed to enjoy for a short while the punishment inflicted on many of its hated politicians. But soon this same anger was directed at the replacements, once the illusions faded and the tremendous deception was fully revealed. Once more in the history of Peru the truth of a statement by Napoleon would be brought out: "Vanity was behind this revolution. Freedom was only a pretext."

Meanwhile, the penetration of areas still not under official control was being consolidated. The government, like all authoritarian governments in Peru, closed in on private institutions. It began with nongovernmental organizations (NGOs) whose resources are now directly controlled by the political power as a result of a government decree stating that all monies not used must be turned back to the government annually. Then there were the professional colleges and organizations: a 1992 law took away their revenues, despite the fact that they were generated privately by the professionals themselves. There is nothing new in all this. Removing areas of freedom and introducing despotism in state-society relations means in Peru carrying out traditional politics. It is a contribution to a perpetuation of despotic government interference in private institutions, and increasing insecurity regarding contractual transactions in civil society. It reinforces the principle that the success of civilian organizations depends on how close they are to the powers that be and that legality is a favor serving to remunerate or offer a payoff in return for a certain political conduct. In certain cases it is simply a form of intimidation.

To "reorganize," for example, the judicial power in relation to the dictates of the national intelligence service as Fujimori has done is not a calling to order of an institution that was obviously highly politicized. It is a further subordinating of justice to political power, a placing of more power in the hands of the central government and robbing civilian society of an instrument that should be a safeguard of its rights even in the face of power itself. Between June and October 1992, the *de facto* government decreed, through the "commission of evaluation" appointed by the executive, the immediate dismissal of 672 members of the judicial power, both magistrates and auxiliaries, among them 100 judges from the Supreme and the Superior Courts, to be replaced by others directly appointed by the government. Not even the Velasco dictatorship had dared, in the 1970s, to brazen through a "remodeling" of the judiciary of this sort.

These antidemocratic practices are something that Peru has experienced under dictatorships as well as democracy. Above all, they are something that the dictatorial republic brought in and that the weak democracies could never change because they had neither the time nor the energy to do what had to be done. Eliminating democratic institutions is not the most rapid route to change: in Peru it means cutting off any possibility of change. And in the 1990 elections a grand mass of Peruvians (80 percent of the voting public), despite a national skepticism regarding politics in general, went to the ballotbox against the slogans of *Sendero Luminoso* and their own disillusion with the ineffectiveness of democratic governments. Eliminating the possibility of a democratic reform is a misreading of our history. Oscar Wilde said that what we must do with history is rewrite it. There is nothing more true in today's Peru, because what our governments, including the current one, have told us is a tremendous contribution to national confusion.

The Peruvian dictatorships, just like elsewhere, have always come up with a justification tied to affairs of national security. In many cases the threat was from abroad. Throughout the past century, after obtaining independence, Peru based a good share of its political identity on an affirmation in the face of a foreign enemy. This enemy was multiform; there were the Spaniards, the Colombians, and the Chileans. Even in this century the Velasco dictatorship took advantage of the nationalist argument. He claimed he was using his betrayal of democracy to save the country from the "hand-over" policies of the first Belaunde government.

The Fujimori coup d'état, as we have seen, is the consequence of a slow process of the military gaining control of institutions, part of the drug dealing power structure and an antidemocratic civilian sector. It also based its actions on the need to preserve national security. But this time it was a case of a domestic threat: *Sendero Luminoso*. Narco traffic was also used as an argument to placate international public opinion and even get financial aid from the United States, which cut off its help as of April 1992 and whose Congress had blocked military aid earlier because of human rights violations. Desperate for income and to revive the antidrug agreement signed in 1991 with the United States, which meant potential economic aid, Fujimori's advisers (among them the dubious figure of Montesinos) brandished the issue of drugs in the face of international, particularly U.S., opinion. This, of course, would block criticism in the international press raining down on the coup government precisely because of its connections with the Alto Huallaga.

But *Sendero Luminoso* was the real card up the sleeve. Along with the fight against corrupt and inept politicians who had spoiled democracy, it was key to the coup makers'arguments. Such reasoning touched a soft spot. The sensation that *Sendero Luminoso* was advancing steadily was invading Peru as well as the international community. According to the Lima-based Human Rights Coordinating Body, the beginnings of the 1990s alone had seen over 3,600 political murders; and the taking over of popular organizations and official institutions by the subversives was felt clearly everyday in the capital and the provinces. International repercussions became a real threat. The murder of Captain Vega Llona in La Paz, Bolivia, in 1988 caused people to suspect that the organization was active there, and seemed to confirm its close contacts with the Bolivian *Tupac Katari* guerrillas, a dissident faction of the *katarista* movement. Several incursions along the Colombian and Chilean borders and even across the border between Bolivia and Argentina had alarmed our South American neighbors. In Peru the idea that a "strong hand" was needed against *Sendero* grew day by day. A climate of ongoing anxiety created by terrorist subversion made it easy to turn the democratic system into a scapegoat of the circumstances with an eye to preserving national integrity. In such an atmosphere it was not difficult to establish a phony hierarchy according to which a democratic system would take second place to the national emergency, as happens in international conflagration. After all, people abroad were speaking of a scenario where in order to detain the overflow of *Sendero*, neighboring armies would make incursions in Peruvian territory. So, in the conscience of the Peruvian political class, domestic and foreign threat became one and the same—a rebirth of an old argument in favor of coups in Peru and elsewhere. Such an argument had a certain echo abroad where it took a number of people in. For example, there was the Federation of American Scientists, which publishes the *Sendero File* under the editorship of Jeremy Stone. In the July and August 1992 editions it showed an alarming naïveté in following the reasoning of the pro-coup government. It attempted to explain that "there had never been real deomcracy" in Peru, leaving the sensation that the 5 April coup had not at all strangled democracy. The international community was vaguely called upon to "pressure Fujimori to maintain democratric procedures." It was falsely affirmed that "over 50 per cent of Peruvian legislators had held their posts for over twenty-five years." This ignored the fact that the parliamentarians of 1980, 1985, and 1990 had been chosen via clean elections, but said nothing of the fact that from 1968 to 1980 there was a military dictatorship ruling without a legislative body.

The argument of national security faced with the *Sendero* threat became the second great justification of the dictatorship. There were few people abroad who answered the call, but at home the argument mobilized survival resources with a mixture of fear and exasperation. The "mystique" of *Sendero* in Peru has had a multiplying effect. Today we know more about this subversive group. But for a long time during the democratic period, which by definition was more open than the dictatorial stage, the insecurity brought about by the fact that *Sendero* was an invisible enemy was added to the exasperation that it had the advantage of penetrating the very mechanisms of a system that in fact it despised. Democracy allowed *Sendero* to infiltrate the organism of the civilized nation like a biological virus. It was like an enemy hiding under the bed.

Who are the *senderistas* and how do they operate? They are a group from the provincial middle class, something which in the old language of the old Peruvians is called *misti*. They emerged from a break between the peasant and indigenous world of their fathers and grandfathers and the provincial urban centers where they emigrated to and found one another. It is a class without roots or land, a social limbo. And to the extent that it no longer belongs to the peasant community, it is without parents. Within the social structure of the provinces they are in fact privileged. But in the difficult provincial capital where they have access to an education offering them arguments to deal politically with their condition they are still newcomers. They are something like transitional men who do not really belong anywhere and are forced to make their way in a world that contemporary Peru has deprived of opportunity and made more and more barren. *Sendero* leader, Abimael Guzmán's condition as an illegitimate son is a metaphor for the social condition of a good part of the *senderistas*. The soil these people treaded was a powder keg that could blow up at any moment.

The first agitation moves by *Sendero* in the Andes were against the education reforms brought in by the Velasco socialist dictatorship. Its struggle against the agrarian reform of the same government in the 1970s indicates a desperate search for identity that finds its expression in the rejection of all manifestations of official policy. The failure of all these reforms and the hatred of official leftism in its journey toward ideological purity lead *Sendero* to armed struggle, a philosophy it adopted in 1976. *Sendero*, then, is the product of an encounter between a déclassé grouping and an education that gave it the privileged tools for intellectual rebellion in the context of a broken society and a failed socialist reform. There was, equally, the frustrated provincial urban centers nourishing their hate of a country with this miserable rural world surrounding them everywhere, which is a humiliating reflection of their own past.

At the beginning of its armed struggle in the 1980s, *Sendero* took full advantage of the resentment of the Andean communities against the farm cooperatives created by agrarian reform in the 1970s in place of the old *haciendas*. The cooperatives incorporated the same peons and employees of the expropriated *haciendas*, but only some of the peasants from the indigenous communities. Lands promised to the latter never became a reality. Property and control of the land was never put into the hands of the peasants in whose name the reforms had been carried out: they remained under the thumb of state bureaucrats. Peasant resentment against this state of affairs was fertile ground for the preaching of *Sendero* when it began its armed actions in the southern Peruvian Andes. At the same time, the subversion managed to link the struggle against all authority and "progress" with the tension between Andean peasants and urban mestizos. So, the guns were aimed at professors, judges, policemen, engineers, and bureaucrats. In time, of course, *Sendero* became for the peasants one more expression of mestizo domination taking over for the previous one even more heavy-handedly. Many people from the provinces began to leave. By 1985 alone some 50,000 people from Ayacucho had fled.

Sendero blocked the slow incorporation of the peasant communities into the market economy, in itself a difficult route owing to the deterrent system successive governments had perpetuated. It operated according to the mistaken premise that the peasant community is a static institution, tied to a subsistence economy and based on exchange and consumption, remote from trade. Reality is much more complex. The communities have preserved such ritual institutions as that of the authority of the *varayoc* (a half-political, half-religious figure), but they struggle to enter the local market economy. *Sendero* interrupted this process wherever it struck. It made token land distributions, but it established a despotic hierarchy and an attack on all forms of social mobility. So there was an evaporation of the initial sympathy generated by the struggle against abusive authorities and rustling and against people taking over neighboring lands. Soon we saw forms of peasant self-defense. The fact is that in much of this Andean territory the Peruvian state scarcely exists, while where it does exist, its presence is suffocating. These self-defense groups were poorly armed and initially failed. When the armed forces would enter a zone, they would not seek the cooperation of local people against *Sendero*, and their indiscriminate brutality made them extremely unpopular. It was only beginning in 1988 that the self-defense patrols, in cooperation with the military, began to grow strong, reaching approximately 100,000 members in the 1990s. So the *Sendero* advance seems to have eased somewhat in recent years in the Andean zone and has concentrated in the country's capital. But it cannot be said that the self-defense partrols and the authorities have pushed *Sendero* back.

While there were almost 8 million Peruvians living under direct military control, in a world where civilian authority is noted for its absence, *Sendero Luminoso* was victorious in its struggle to denounce democracy as a masquerade of repressive and authoritarian forces. Attacks in these years have not decreased either. In 1992, extensive parts of the central sierra and the southern area of the country were under *Sendero's* control.

Beginning in 1985 statistics show that there were more terrorist attacks in Lima than in Ayacucho, and that the surrounding of the capital was intensified. This process had been going on for several years. Journalist Michael Smith has demonstrated how the insurgents penetrated in the Ate-Vitarte zone, east of Lima, in a complex undertaking that included land takeovers, the capture of populist assemblies, and an infiltration of trade union movements.[5] This Lima zone is on the edge of the Central Highway, amid what is considered the industrial corridor of the capital. Passing through is the central railway and the road linking the Callao Port with the Rímac River, the extension of which ties Lima to the central sierra. This is the strategic center providing water and electrical energy. The hydroelectric and thermal energy plant there supplies some 70 percent of Lima's needs. The rest comes from transmission lines stretching from the Mantaro Valley in the central sierra of Junín all the way to Lima. The Central Highway is the link between the two zones, and through it foodstuffs travel to the capital. A sharp sense of strategic logic told *Sendero Luminoso* to worm its way into that zone, something expressed only in part in multiple attacks against high-tension towers and the taking over of extensions of the highway through which food goes to the city. As important as these actions has been the taking over of trade unions established in this economic bastion of the country (Lima makes up 70 percent of Peru's manufacturing capacity). *Sendero Luminoso's* Metropolitan Committee is responsible for the Lima zone and equivalent to the hierarchy operating in Ayacucho, the cradle of subversion, ranking above other regional committees. As such it has, since the end of the 1980s, constantly penetrated grass-roots organizations like the Glass of Milk Program, Popular Kitchens, evangelical groups, political parties, along with temporary employment and humanitarian assistance programs. Via elections, the *Sendero* people have reached positions of control in many grass-roots organizations; and in other cases its members have simply intimidated the leaders into submission. For example, in Villa El Salvador, a huge shantytown on the outskirts of the capital with several hundred thousand inhabitants, many organizations have been taken over by the subversives, like the Federation of Women, which supervises the distribution of milk, and the Federation of Small Business-men. But most important here is CUAVES (Comunidad Urbana Autoges-tionaria), the main communal body. In its fourth convention held in August 1992 under the dictatorship of Alberto Fujimori, with the consent of the terrorized general secretary of CUAVES, Filadelfo Roa, the *senderistas* led by Raúl Maguina imposed and wrote up the conclusions of the meeting; that is, they established the entire action plan for the year.

In many cases *Sendero* uses pure criminality in its attacks on grass-roots institutions. During the 1991-92 period twenty leaders in San Juan de Lurigancho—another large town south of Lima, a product of migra-tions to the city in recent decades—were murdered by the terrorists. The most spectacular and moving murder of a grass-roots figure came with the case of María Elena Moyano in February 1992. She was a much admired leader as head of the women's organization and other com-munity groups. Her death made the country shudder.

In 1989 *Sendero* carried to Lima a struggle tactic it had used time and time again in the provinces: the "armed strike," a forced strike under the threat of violence against anyone who attempts to work. In the 1980s, an economic crisis that cut industrial production by one-half devastated the masses of people living in the outskirts of Lima, rendering desperate the situation of the employed and the underemployed in the capital. Many doors that the peasants fleeing to Lima hoped to find open were closed. *Sendero* grew in this climate of hopelessness. In the 1990s there began a new tactical turn on the part of the subversives: social aid. They asked for and contributed to the establishment of social services in the new communities, at the same time using terror to paralyze average citizens. In several cases, in the town of Raucana near the Central Highway, for example, in July 1990, *Sendero* managed to control completely the population by offering them access to land it had confiscated.

You could say that in these years only one piece of evidence was left of the Peruvians' will to resist the evil force of *Sendero Luminoso*. It was the massive participation in the presidential, legislative, and municipal elections. By contrast, all other civilian activity offered a sense of resignation. Even in the elections there were indications that the subver-sives had gained ground among the population. In the first electoral round in 1990 the number of blank ballots rose to the alarming level of 15 percent. The level of absenteeism in such emergency zones as Huánuco, Ayacucho, and Junín came to almost 50 percent. In the southern sierra of the country half of the eligible voters had followed *Sendero*'s instructions. In the rest of the country the vast majority voted.

It is calculated that *Sendero*'s army is made up of over 20,000 people. But the sporadic nature of armed actions, their constant passing from underground to daily city life and then back into hiding, the existence of mobile cells that are unconnected, and committees with a high degree of autonomy in different zones make for a nonconventional force. Their apocalyptic ideology gives them great determination and a capacity to resist any adversary. And at points where part of the main leadership has been done away with (the prison murders of 1986, for example), it has not taken long to rebuild morale and the chain of command. *Sendero*'s ideology seeks to transplant a number of Maoist postulates to Peru, a place having little to do with China at the beginning of the century when the people of Mao began their long march to power. In the first place, China was scarcely 10 percent urban and overwhelmingly rural. Recent decades have seen Peru take a tremendous turn: today it is 70 percent urban. China was semifeudal, while imperialist invasions had introduced forms of capitalism that only partly modified the system and did not radically alter structures in the country. In Peru, feudalism, which was waning anyway, ended with the socialism of Velasco Alvarado who did away with the *haciendas* and their owners. The semicolonial situation China underwent with foreign armies in its soil is not that of Peru, a country that has been independent since the last century. In China only 10 percent of the population could read and write, whereas illiterates have always been a minority in Peru. So it is not similarities between China and Peru that offer the Maoist message its strength. It is rather the apocalyptic vision in the preaching of the *Sendero* people and, above all, the violent methods of struggle that have taken advantage of the weakness of our civilian institutions as they worm their way in and bring them down internally. Apart from a political similarity between the minute international revolutionary movement of Maoists and the efficient propaganda of the *Sendero* committees in Europe and the United States, links between Peruvian subversion and forces abroad do not exist.

Subversion took a spectacular leap during the Alberto Fujimori government, despite growing militarization in 1990 and 1991. In the twenty months preceding the coup d'état political violence brought about

6,700 deaths, over two-thirds of the number who died during Alan García's entire reign. In 1991 *Sendero* announced it had achieved what it considered "strategic parity" in its confrontation with the state. Thus, when Fujimori justified his coup with talk about a lack of action on the part of the politicians against *Sendero*, he was actually indulging in very serious self-criticism. The fact is that his own weakness in facing down *Sendero*, despite the militarization that his government speeded up as of July 1990, was responsible for what was going on. After the coup he continued to emphasize militarization.

The capture of the founder and leader of *Sendero Luminoso*, Abimael Guzmán, took place on 12 September 1992. This was and was not by chance. The chance factor was in the date. The fact that Fujimori's coup was quite recent seemed to indicate that the current system was efficient in beating back subversion. What was not by chance was the fact that it was the National Bureau Against Terrorism (DINCOTE), the police, that on 12 September finally discovered the whereabouts of Abimael Guzmán. This special body had defended—according to the philosophy of its chief, General Antonio Vidal—intelligence work as opposed to blind military repression. So much so that in 1990 this had angered adviser Vladimiro Montesinos. As a result of the tension, Fujimori's military advisers had reduced DINCOTE's budget, despite the fact that the police had already shown signs of efficiency. Under the Fujimori government they had discovered several *Sendero* hideouts in residential areas of the capital along with documents leading to the arrest of important members of the Metropolitan Committee. One of the discoveries was an important videotape where Guzmán appears celebrating with his underlings. It is a bizarre bacchanalian ceremony including what some observers have called a "Greek dance."

Up to the arrest of Guzmán, and despite the fact that the government was acting outside the law as of April 1992, *Sendero* had stepped up its activities. That period witnessed 22 car bombs, a 1000 people injured, $250 million in damages, and 12 explosive devices that authorities were able to deactivate. In July there was the "armed strike," which paralyzed the fleet of 7,000 buses providing transport for the citizens of the capital. The most traumatic terrorist attacks came during the dictatorial government. In the first week of July 600 kilos of dynamite were used to blow up the headquarters of a television station (Channel 2) in Lima. This was the beginning of *Sendero*'s use of truck bombs, something they had not done before. Ironically, the truck in question had been stolen from the navy. On 16 July 1,000 kilos of dynamite divided into two bombs went off on Tarata Street in the Miraflores district, while twenty-five other explosive devices spread terror throughout the rest of Lima. The attack on Miraflores brought the middle-class neighborhoods into a war from which they thought they were largely exempt, even though there had been minor and sporadic attacks before, like the blowing up of banks, embassies, and public buildings. On 20 July 300 kilos of dynamite went off at the Institute of Liberty and Democracy. That same day, 100 kilometers from the capital on the Central Highway, the Infiernillo Bridge was blown apart. It was obvious that *Sendero* had qualitatively increased its level of urban subversion and was making a serious offensive on the capital in open defiance of the coup d'état.

But not even the arrest of Abimael Guzmán removed the feeling that *Sendero* was proceeding with its murderous campaign. In September 1992 alone there were 182 attacks: an average of 6 daily. It was the most violent month of the year. Of the 182 attacks, 108 came in Lima where in theory violence should have diminished because of the military mobilization in the streets and outskirts, and the indiscriminate searching of homes and public institutions. And not even in the sierra was there a lessening of attacks: 57 attacks took place there that same month. The rest were in the jungle zone, in the east of Peru. In September there were 216 victims: 42 from shantytowns, 28 students, 80 workers, 11 leaders of grass-roots organizations, 8 professionals, 7 merchants, and the rest peasants, police, and army people, in short, a broad cross section of citizens. Toward the end of 1992 Abimael Guzmán and several members of the Metropolitan Committee were in jail. Among the latter was its chief, Gilberto Iparraguirre, arrested as well thanks to the hard intelligence work of DINCOTE. Also behind bars was the leader of *Movimiento Revolucionario Tupac Amaru* (MRTA), Víctor Polay, who turned himself over to authorities in July 1992. But Fujimori's claim that terrorism was about to be liquidated still did not seem to be based on solid ground. The Human Rights Commission of Peru (*Comisión de Derechos Humanos del Perú*) stated that there were some 1,500 terrorist attacks during all of 1992, half of which were commited by *Sendero*.

The capture of Guzmán was without a doubt an extremely hard blow for the subversives. *Sendero* is a disciplined hierarchical movement. It has a vertical structure with the leader wielding all the organization's ideological, moral, and political power. However, in recent times *Sendero*'s regional committees had acted with a good deal of autonomy. While Guzmán set the ideological and political tone, the daily struggle was rather independent of the leader himself. This seemed to be confirmed by events during the months after his capture. Nearing the elections for the Constituent Assembly set for 22 November, *Sendero Luminoso* started a terror campaign in Lima perfectly reminiscent of those undertaken during its most intense militaristic period. On 18 November they called an "armed strike," which paralyzed the capital, and on that same day twenty bombs were set off in Lima, including one in Miraflores, where a deadful terrorist attack had been carried out not long before. In order to mount a successful "armed strike" in Lima a very well established and widely distributed organization was needed. *Sendero* announced, therefore, that, despite the fall of its leader, its organization was alive and well. In addition, there was the maladroit use by the government of Guzmán behind bars for television purposes and then the shady proceedings by an invisible military tribunal, along with a speech by Fujimori offering a summary sentence even before any trial had taken place. This total lack of respect for the rule of law supported the *Sendero* assertion that they were fighting a system with no legitimacy. In this way, an attempt to strip Guzmán of his mystique and make him seem like a common madman became a masquerade of justice completely in line with *Sendero*'s reasoning. This does not obscure the fact that Guzmán is mainly responsible for the political violence since 1980 whose cross fire has caused 25,000 lives and around $30 billion in material damages.

Fujimori's new antiterrorist approach was rooted in a just principle, giving back a judicial system, which in previous years had freed almost 200 *senderistas*, its raison d'être and authority. But what was established was a completely unjust system: summary trials by invisible courts, no witnesses, no appeals. The weight of the new government philosophy fell on prisons as well. In May 1992 Fujimori ordered the transfer of women accused of terrorism from the Castro Castro Centre to another set up near the Santa Mónica Centre in Chorrillos. This one did not fall under the authority of the director of the Santa Mónica Centre, but directly under that of the Government Palace. Visitors (including those from human rights groups) and the distribution of food and medicine from family members were forbidden. In October 1992 the government, announced it would denounce the Costa Rica agreements on human rights that prohibited the death penalty. It wanted to establish capital punishment as soon as possible in Peru and apply it retroactively (a violation of legal norms) to *Sendero* leaders already sentenced. The whole process became a Roman circus when in the same month Fujimori announced his intention to call a general referendum on a death sentence for Abimael Guzmán. This would mean a new sentence, issued by the masses, overruling the one brought down by the invisible military court.

The coup d'état interrupted a process that was underway in the marginal zones of Lima following the death of María Elena Moyano. There had been a growing cooperation between the population and the authorities in the fight against *Sendero*. This spontaneous effort on the part of the people, from the base to the top, had been nonexistent for some years and its absence had constituted the greatest failure in the antisubversive strategy of the authorities. But as of the installation of the de facto regime it came to be substituted by unilateral action on the part of the armed forces imposed from above within a military type of organization. The populist element used by the government to soften the blow—the distribution of donations by army convoys—has not been enough to establish that voluntary complicity between grass-roots organizations and the central power. Without it the government might wipe *MRTA* (a small and typically Castroite organization) off the face of the Peruvian map, but hardly *Sendero*.

It is very difficult to establish clearly the impact of the arrest of Guzmán and the various *Sendero* cohorts. This was really the work of a police institution distanced from the Government Palace and the mandates of the all-powerful Montesinos. If the measure of success in the struggle against terror is the total number of attacks, subsequent months are no cause for optimism, despite government claims. This should not be the yardstick; there is something else. I agree with journalist, Gustavo Gorriti, in his studies of the *Sendero* phenomenon, when he says the benchmark for success in combating *Sendero* should be the amount of Peruvian territory recaptured by civilian authority and legality. According to this criterion, *Sendero Luminoso* continues to win overwhelmingly. The territory under military control since 5 April has increased systematically, a system based on force and not legality. There is endless evidence through the years of a lack of effectiveness of the military option in the battle against *Sendero* subversion. In the province of La Mar alone, in Ayacucho, 10 percent of the population (some 10,000 people) have been killed under military authority; but subversion continues there. On 30 October 1992, several months after the coup, we saw one of the most savage terrorist attacks in that southern Andean zone. It took the lives of eleven people. Ayacucho has been under military rule for several years.

The deep-rooted causes of violence will not disappear with the dictatorship. These are: social dislocation, the survival of a system that hinders the majority from creating wealth and condemns them to seeking out ways of survival that might be imaginative but do not put prosperity into many hands, and the absence of an integrating market for this mosaic of cultures and races under an administration of justice that protects the weak as well as the strong. The dictatorship can stop *Sendero's* purely military advance for a certain period of time (and it does not seem like this is happening); but as long as this is the work of a regime without legitimacy, *Sendero Luminoso*, which had been denouncing the democratic system since 1980 as a farce and a fraud, continues to win out. What exists in Peru is not the system (feudal, colonial, capitalist) against which *Sendero* is struggling; but neither is it remotely a just, open, clean, modern, and civil system for which many have struggled in recent years against subversion and terrorism in the name of democracy. As long as the degeneration of civilian ways of coexistence continues and Peru is divided into areas controlled by *Sendero Luminoso* (though they be a minority) and those controlled by the military, all Peruvians will be losing the fight for democracy.

Notes

1. *Criollos* were the descendants of Spaniards born in the Spanish colonies. Developing a taste for independence, they fought off colonial rule.
2. Jorge Basadre, *Perú: problema y posibilidad*, 2d ed. (Lima: Banco Internacional, 1978).
3. The *Guano*, or bird manure, became Peru's principal economic asset during much of the last century thanks to Western demand for its fertilizing properties.
4. Persecution of journalists reached alarming proportions during 1992. Jail sentences were given to César Hildebrandt, Enrique Zileri, Cecilia Valenzuela, Danilo Quijano and Ricardo Uceda, and the bank accounts of Francisco Igartua's *Oiga* magazine were immobilized by the government. But not only journalists have been savagely persecuted. In July 1993 the dictatorship killed one of the few movements of resistance against the régime, when the Mayor of Chiclayo, Arturo Castillo Chirinos, was sentenced to four years in prison by the Superior Court of Lambayeque. Chirinos was the leader of AMPE, a movement of Peruvian mayors created in 1993 to oppose the government, which had become the main civilian threat to Fujimori.

Following a procedure used against many others, a non-existant organization sued Chirinos for apparent irregularities in the administration of funds provided by the central government. When two judges acquitted Chirinos of any wrongdoing, Fujimori ordered a reopening of the case and obtained the jail sentence he wanted.

5. Michael L. Smith, "Shining Path's Urban Strategy: Ate Vitarte," in *Shining Path of Peru*, edited by David Scott Palmer (New York: St. Martin's Press, 1992).

3

The Origins of Misery

Mr. Buenaventura Huamani manages one of Lima's small groceries stores where many Peruvians make their living. He has bulging cheekbones, a squashed nose, and a lot of thick hair. He wants to leave the country, so he pays a visit to Master Fujimoto's clinic: "Full treatment, please." Master Fujimoto puts the patient on a bed in a shabby room in the center of the city where he also earns his living. Several hours later, Huamani awakens feeling like a new man. He still has bulging cheekbones, a squashed nose, and a lot of thick hair—but there's something new: he has slanted eyes. With them (better than with the birth certificate of some far-off relative) this gentleman can visit the Japanese consulate in Lima, claim ancestry in the Land of the Rising Sun, and undertake proceedings that will hopefully give him a tourist visa so he can go to the land of his forebears and gather papers for citizenship. By the time authorities become aware of the slick trick, Huamani will already be there mixed with the Phillipinos and Arabs, one among the many in the crowd of the underground economy, in a geography that he would not be able to spot on a map, learning a mysterious language, and experiencing a culture gap broader than the whole Pacific Ocean. He will perhaps be ignorant of the commonly accepted theory that situates his far-off ancestors among Asians who during the final glacial era crossed Siberia and the Bering Straits aboard ice floes, which were probably more substantial than the caravels of Christopher Columbus.

This is one among the thousand faces adopted by today's Peruvian picaresque in the plight against general hopelessness. Like Huamani, many humble and not so humble Peruvians slant their eyes in order to escape to Japan. It is not a fashion emerging from the Japanese origins of Mr. Alberto Fujimori. This may have accelerated the phenomenon, but it is really part of a broader reality: emigration. One of the traits of Peru's precolonial past was the violent transfer of population by the Inca state. Colonialism continued this tradition. Today population movements, within Peru and abroad, are voluntary. Between 1987 and 1992, according to a study by Peruvian anthropologist Teófilo Altamirano, 235,000 people fled from poverty and violence in Peru. This brings the total of exiled Peruvians to one 1.1 million. Between 1985 and 1990, 11,000 professionals, 3,500 technicians, 3,000 businessmen, and 27,000 students migrated to the United States, the preferred destination of these fugitives, followed by Spain, Chile, Japan, Canada, and Australia. This involves a significant percentage of current and future leaders. The bulk of the emigrants, of course, belong to the country's poorer sectors, from the middle class down. The great phenomenon of domestic country-city migration in recent decades in Peru has come to be overtaken by that of international emigration. The lines of a famous Peruvian waltz go: "Those crazy dreams of mine/ took me away from my village/ and I abandoned my turf/ for the capital to see." Today Peruvian decadence has turned that capital, which used to be a point of destination, into a place of departure.

Such statistical reality offers only a vague idea of the hopeless atmosphere in which Peruvian politics was taking place in recent times, the context of Fujimori's rise to power, and the kind of country where the dictatorial metamorphosis of the regime occurred. The reasons for such a decadence are not immediately obvious. They are anchored in Peru's historical experience, in the inveterate political characteristics of our state, beginning with the dawn of civilization in Peruvian territory, some 900 years B.C. among the astonishing members of the Chavín culture, all the way up to modern times, passing through a multitide of epochs— the pre-Inca, the Inca, the colonial, and the republican. Each one of these added a new dimension to the inheritance of the past, but was unable to blend it with the legacy of earlier epochs. Instead of filling the gaps, they offered different forms of the same evils.

One has to dig deep into history in order to understand how Peru has come to its current crisis. Without this it is impossible to comprehend, for example, the blind and irresponsible voting of 1990, or to grasp the majority popular backing (by no means as great as the first surveys in April 1992 claimed: 98 percent in favor) of Fujimori's coup d'état. Without such wider vision it is impossible to understand how sectors that seemed firmly on the side of democracy—from the business class to the mass media, who did not have the excuse of ignorance or hopelessness that might be claimed by more humble Peruvians—came to betray a system that they had claimed to defend for twelve years. Moreover, these sectors had been the main victims of the dictatorship of the 1970s. Among the many symbols of this attitude is a communiqué issued on 7 April by CONFIEP, the main business organization, which was extremely supportive of the coup. The editor of *El Comercio*, the most prestigious daily in the country, welcomed Fujimori warmly in his office while military censors with machine guns were sweeping the press rooms. There is also the case of *Expreso*, whose editor, the day after the presidential visit to *El Comercio*, asked to receive equal treatment. Faust sold his soul to the devil in exchange for earthly pleasure: Peru's ruling class sold their souls on 5 April with no real guarantee of anything. Nothing at all is certain in the slippery political world of today's Peru. Experience shows, moreover, that once the popularity of a dictatorial regime evaporates (dictatorships are never unpopular at the beginning), the precarious base of support of the government can fall appart at any moment.

The phenomenon of this dual Peru, the ragged and the ruling class, converging in a strange coincidence in favor of a dictatorial cause can only be understood by studying in Peruvian history that sequence of frustrations, gaps, violence, and perseverances that have created today's circumstances and that are responsible for the two poles of Peruvian life. Without this it is impossible to understand, for example, the posture of Peru's business community. They went like tigers in the name of democracy for Alan García's jugular vein when he tried to confiscate private banks in 1987, after falling at his feet for two years. Then they collaborated decisively in bringing that democracy down, failing to understand that they were the sons of the old republican mercantilism responsible for Peru's crisis. The mercantilist system has a long history behind it. It gained strength with a small clique of businessmen, which articulated itself during last century around *guano* and later around cotton and sugar, and which, more recently, was carried on, in the 1920s, with the emergence of industry, under Augusto Leguía, in the 1940s and 1950s under Manuel Prado and Manuel Odría, and later on under subsequent governments.

We have a ruling class that never learned that the real wealth and integration of a society grow to the extent that those on the fringe can grasp the forbidden fruit—law, property, business, power—they never enjoyed before. One can almost understand, because of so desperate a condition, the political response emerging in the 1990s from the silent majority that one day decided to speak. However, it is still painful to witness that historical lack of national consciousness concerning the traditional causes of the Peruvian disaster and the mixture of hatred, fears, and sophisms that have surfaced and that contribute in a negative way to the shaping of today's dramatic political phemonena.

Among the middle and lower classes, massive emigration abroad and the political behavior in voting for an unknown like Alberto Fujimori and then later backing the coup d'état are expressions of a frustration with the country and its institutions. Through very different routes and for different reasons the leading class and the masses on the fringe converged temporarily behind the Peruvian government's authoritarian project. They were convinced that democracy is not worthwhile, despite the fact that the word means something different for each. And there are differences too in the flaws attributed to democracy by both sides, and in the way this political system touched their everyday lives in the 1980s. This is a story that began a long time ago and has to do with failed relations between State and civil society from the beginning up until today. There has been an inability to create legitimate and authentically democratic institutions really national in scope and nature that might integrate the cultural and racial mosaic making up Peru and overcome the fissures in its history.

For a long time, in the eyes of the world, the Incas monopolized Peru's past. This was historical blindness. The Incas were only the culmination of a much earlier and longer process. Their empire was relatively short-lived, lasting not more than 100 years. In the centuries dividing the earliest important civilization (over 900 years B.C.) and the Spanish conquest of the Inca empire in the sixteenth century of our era, we can trace the remote roots of the Peruvian state and, in more tenuous forms, the origins of a civil society. Both state and society changed so much with the arrival of the white man that it would not be difficult to call them unrecognizable today, although there are clear traces of the ancient culture in the 85 percent of the Peruvian population made up of Indians and mestizos. But there is not only a race, arts and crafts, and a very minor form of agriculture surviving. Something of a sediment of the

Peruvian society and state before the Spanish conquest is still very strongly present.

The Chavín culture took shape as a civilization after a long prehistoric evolution of Indian nomads coming from Central America who, at the dawn of the neolithic age, had discovered agriculture and become sedentary. For nearly half a millennium this culture expanded throughout the country, covering various regions, from the coast to the mountains and from north to south, always within a cultural unity. These people constituted, together with the Tiahuanaco, born some 500 years A.D., the spinal column of the indigenous world prior to the Incas. They contributed immensely to the forming of an era and a multitude of other cultures, some local, like Lima and Cajamarca, and some more ambitious like Paracas, Nazca, and Mochica. Their art is a testimony to a religion, an economy, and a society.

There was no market economy as such before the Incas. But in a deformed manner there was a sort of modern institution: private property. There was the *ayllu*, an agrarian community of one or more families that claimed to descend from some remote divinity, spread throughout the vertical geography of the Andes. Barter and exchange were the instruments for obtaining goods or labor. The families owned the land, not the state (which did not yet exist). The places where the natives lived and their work implements were private property. There was a hierarchy, at the top of which was the *curaca*. He had workers to satisfy his needs, greater than those of the rest of the community, and he was the link between man and the world beyond the community. But his authority was not untouchable: it came from a consensus of the community. He had to earn the right to be the chief by demonstrating his family ties with the rest of the group and his economic contribution in exchange for what he received within a principle of reciprocity. His responsibilities included defending the community against the incursions of rivals, giving as many gifts as he received, distributing land, and seeing to the protection of everyone's property. One could say that at that time the legitimacy of civil authority rested upon a political consensus, and authority as such was limited by society. Jean-Jacques Rousseau, who was not exactly a liberal, gave a brilliant definition of the birth of civil society: "*The first man who, after having fenced off his land, lays claim to it is the real founder of civil society.*" Peru, which was not yet Peru, already had a civil society. There was no market in that world, but there was private property and competition, characterized by a multitude of conflicts among neighboring communities and the fact that they all had different levels of wealth.

Knowing this is a relief for someone who loves liberty, because for many years Marxist propaganda cultivated the idea that precolonial Peru was an ideal communist society. This is false. It was certainly not a modern civil society either. The Collas, the Huancas, the Chimúes, among others, were peoples with tribal systems, or feudal systems where the power of the *curaca* was greatest, resembling the beginnings of the European Middle Ages more than the communism of our century. But they were rather less seignorial than the former and with a greater sense of participation of the individual and the family in decisions having to do with general surroundings and more limits to authority. One must not idealize this world; it was violent and static. But within it we find the rudiments of a civil society that the Peruvian state, as soon as the Inca empire was established, destroyed.

The Inca empire was born of migrations along the Urubamba in the Cuzco zone during the twelfth century; but it was only at the end of the first quarter of the fifteeth century that it established its hegemony outside the zone. The Incas were not described this way for a long time by American, European, and Latin American intellectuals, out to compare and humble the work of Western culture with utopian examples of a supposed Peruvian past. But the Incas were indeed a great civilization. Spreading throughout the South American continent, they constructed roads and bridges and irrigation systems that were marvels to behold. They raised monuments and worked precious metals in splendid artistic forms. But they offered Peruvian life for the first time a society at the service of the state. One can still see the traces of this tragedy today, even though the essential outlines of Peru's current state come mainly from the republican and, to a certain extent, colonial eras. A large degree of state organization during the colonial period was carried out on a greater scale in Peru than in other parts of the colonial empire precisely because it had been the center of a powerful pre-Columbian culture that had to be replaced. Countries like Chile, on the periphery of the Inca empire, did not have to experience the enormous weight of the colonial state that Peru suffered, to a large extent because it never had the imperial system we went through under the Incas.

The Incas did have the good sense to preserve the *ayllu* system. But the holding of land was under the control of the emperor who gave it temporarily to the communities. This spoiled the *ayllu* and turned it into an institution serving the state. A system was established by which, with the exception of those strictly necessary for survival, all crops belonged to the state. This was organized to cover the needs of the vast ruling class—priests, functionaries, noblemen—and the rest went to support religion and fill the stocks *(tambos)*, which were kept in case of war or natural catastrophe. It is unfortunate that from such a structure, based on a subjection of society to state, the only worthwhile principle has not survived to our days: that of the *tambos*. Our republican system has nurtured, from time to time, considerable deficits.

One had to work the land assigned him by the state and limit himself to using officially issued goods for daily necessities. The state worked its way into society implanting a system of forced distribution of the population. The idea was to break down local resistance to the new empire system and disperse individuals imbued with the new philosophy who could influence the local population. This dislocation of people also had to do with other state interests: many residents were removed from their lands to serve the dominant class, to labor in vast public projects derived from the imperial philosophy or to work in the mines. The Inca establishment stimulated a functionary culture that is still one of Peru's greatest problems. The supervision of the activities of the people was tough, and the accounting of the empire was detailed. In addition the Incas established a society-power relationship emerging apart from the principle of equality. In order to conquer more territory and offer the empire more breathing space, the Incas worked out short-term alliances with neighboring peoples whom they paid back for subjecting others. When any of the latter threatened to become too rebellious, the process was reversed and there was an alliance with another group of Indians.

The Peruvian state as such, then, not only grew intolerably in numbers, space, and interference in that century of imperial domination. It also laid the foundations for a permanent distortion of relationships between the state and civilian society, establishing the beginnings of a system of privilege and discrimination, of exclusive interest groups depending on state favor. The power of the state came to be, not the guarantor of social life, but its rotation axis, like the sun in relation to its satellites. A heliocentric state was born in Peru, and this was also in the literal sense, because the Incas, beginning with Manco Cápac, considered themselves descendants of the sun. To this all-powerful state there was added the figure of the patriarch, the emperor, the owner of everything. This is another inheritance that drags on through our days. Our republican *caudillos* have acted as though Peru were in some way their fief, their property, their patrimony. In Peru, the patrimonial state, which Mexican poet Octavio Paz has spoken about in reference to Latin American states in general, has its roots among the Incas.

These features remained alive and expanded during the colonial period with the arrival of the Spaniards and *conquistador* Francisco Pizarro in the sixteenth century. Soon the foundations of the Inca establishment suffered the consequences of the very lack of stability of a system of temporary and shaky alliances between the state and various peoples. We cannot understand the conquest of the vast Inca empire by a handful of Spaniards without taking into account the collaboration of peoples like the Huancas. The vision of a unitary pre-colonial world with a "national consciousness" or an "Indian consciousness" is completely false. No such thing existed. The consciousness continued to be tribal. The *ayllu* did suffer the devastating consequences of state penetration; but it continued to exist as a social rite and an autarchical custom. The fact is that the indigenous community whose roots are linked to Peru's prehistory subsists even today in the Andes scattered among some 4,000 units. It is the only witness to the totality of our history and a true bridge in time between our different historical stages. The lack of national consciousness—perfectly understandable among communities with old autarchical customs and subjected to centralist despotism—allowed the Spaniards to take over the territory with relative ease once they had captured the Inca Atahualpa in Cajamarca. The vertical nature of the Inca system, as we have seen, is not alien to our times; and its weakness was revealed then. Lacking the centripetal force of the emperor, the empire fell apart. Although for many years there were attempts to beat back the Spaniards and re-establish the rule of the Incas, the colonial rule took over Peru for three centuries. This new historical phase perpetuated many deficiencies, weaknesses, and inequalities of state-civil society relationships, and added more.

The experience decisively forging contemporary Peru, without underplaying the pre-colonial and republican stages, is the conquest and the colony. The political organization implanted by the white man (the

Spaniard) and the juridical patterns that ruled civilian society for three centuries—economic activities, social hierarchy, relations with power and with itself—decisively marked Peru and created institutions that the republic, with all its newness, has really never been able to overcome. The Spain that conquered Peru was not the England of the Stuarts, the colonists, and the Reformation. It was the bastion of the Counter-Reformation and of absolutism, the head of a shocking empire that with Charles V was out to make the new lands an extension of its own European structure. This meant the transplanting of existing institutions and the creation of new ones, which, reflecting the characteristics of the empire, absorbed the native peoples. In a place like Peru, creator of its own structure of civilization, this implied a trauma. The result was an inorganic, dual, disintegrated, and violent world, a sort of quicksand where it was practically impossible to form a stable institution because reality questioned them and overcame them constantly.

The political order created by the conquest built on some inheritances, among them, rivalries between the Indians. There emerged stronger than before a system by which the conquerers and the conquered exchanged privileges in return for assistance and, especially, labor. The major agents of the alliances of the conquerors and the communities were, of course, the *curacas*. Pizarro's men knew full well that it would be impossible to control the territory, resist permanent threats of aggression and secure a work force without alliances. The *curacas* came to understand in many communities that closeness to power offered many privileges; and the Spaniards governed in this way for many years. Pizarro gave *encomiendas* to his fellow Spaniards, an institution that would last throughout the colonial period. By means of the *encomienda* the *conquistador* took a certain number of Indians into his custody. He had to provide for them, and they had to work for him. The link between the *conquistadores* and the *encomiendas* were once again the *curacas*. In exchange for favors they organized the slow but steady passage of the population of the communities to this new form of domination. In many cases the *curaca* stopped being an expression of the indigenous community and became an instrument of power. This perversion lasts until today. The equivalent figure in our times is the *cacique* or local boss, the real master of the provinces, who uses extortion, corruption, brute force, and charity in order to obtain political and economic power in the region in question and become a link with the outside world.

The Spanish crown crushed all possibilities of the *encomienda* becoming a form of decentralized, autonomous, and regional power capable of laying the foundations of a state with such characteristics, so necessary in a country with such different peoples and a vast distribution of natural resources. The *encomienda* was not slavery; it was without a doubt an aberrant form of domination. But among the different forms of organization the conquest might have adopted it was the farthest from monarchic absolutism, a system a little more like the mitigated feudalism at the end of the European Middle Ages, responsible to a large extent for the collapse on that continent of monarchic absolutism and the emergence of a new order.

In Peru the Hapsburgs reacted against the decentralized forms of organization, not only against the *encomienda* but also against an institution that could have been essential when it came to creating forms of power really in touch with the common people: the *cabildo* or city council. From the beginning, the crown limited its functions and stifled its budget. It made its authorities, the *regidores* or councillors , into pompous, arrogant, and purely superficial figures alienated from the community. The *cabildo* should have been the strongest political expression of all the cities founded by the Spaniards. But it was not.

The power of the crown, which was linked to the colonies through the figure of the viceroy, could not totally stamp out the development of these regional institutions. The result of the conflict was a new political perversion that still exists today: a permanent transaction between power and subject aimed at forcing the law. The *encomenderos* offered the crown gifts in exchange for privileges in order to perpetuate the original institutions of the conquest, but in a deformed way, depending not on the established legal regime but on an ongoing pact with power. And they were limited regarding their capacity for development. This practice, of course, was extended throughout the indigenous population. Since the crown was the protector of the Indians, they called frequently, with donations, on the sensibility of royal power in Lima and the metropolis for special concessions.

This was a form of defending themselves against the abuses of the Spaniards in the colony. But it is also very clear that the conception of power-society relationships depended on the ability of the subject to gratify authorities so that they might act on one's behalf instead of defending commonly respected (feared or hated) legislation. This system saw to it that the law (for Spaniards as well as Indians) did not have a general, abstract, and permanent nature. It was specific, individual and whimsical. The crown, which at home had suppressed religious, regional, and municipal liberties, tried to quash the autonomy of the *conquistadores* and the *encomiendas* in the colonies, but was not successful. The result was a transaction: the patrimonial state. The king was the owner of everything—the lands, the mines, and the *obrajes* (textile plants), which the *conquistadores* administered in his name. He owned the Indians who worked in these places and the legislation, by way of the *Consejo de Indias* the institution in charge of the administrative and economic affairs of the colonies.

The system that the conquest implanted was that of a patrimonial, centralized, and mercantilist state; but it was not feudal, as so many have claimed. The *encomiendas*, and later on the *haciendas* of the colonies, were not feudal estates. The central state intervened to block the absolute power of the masters and to mitigate servitude. The *encomiendas* by no means emcompassed the better part of the land and were influenced by capitalist activities in the cities and ports. They were part of a system depending directly on the central state. The world of the *hacienda* and the mine was semifeudal to the extent that it favored agriculture and mining at the expense of trade and industry; but forms of capitalism were budding throughout the colony, and they spread their influence up and down the territory.

The type of capitalism in question has deeply marked the Peruvian economy. It was the worst sort of capitalism, made of monopolies, prohibitions, controls, excessive rules and regulations, and a rentier economy; and from that emerged smuggling, corruption, and the creation of small oligarchies excluding the vast majority from the market. The major source of wealth were the mines discovered in the sixteenth century. The crown took them over and exploited them tirelessly, although Peru also exported potatoes, corn, sugar, and textiles. Mining was a source of income, but not of authentic capitalist development. The sluggish system of the mining economy meant, for example, that the Spaniards did not introduce the use of steam engines for quite some time. Silver and gold were shipped to Spain via Panama, and the same route was used to supply the colonies with products from the metropolis. Via Mexico there was trade with the Philippines, another Spanish colony. The ports were monopolies on both sides of the Atlantic. A small group of businessmen belonging to the Consulship Tribunal in Lima (*Tribunal del Consulado*) had control of all trade. The Peruvian and Spanish traders often came to agreements to restrict the flow of merchandise so that prices would rise. Of course trade with other European countries was forbidden, although a number of foreigners managed to work their way into the commercial world of the colony.

From the beginning the response was smuggling, a prosperous and permanent institution during the colonial days. Here there was wide participation of Englishmen, Frenchmen, Dutchmen, and even Spaniards. The Spanish authorities themselves were quite often accomplices in the ongoing circumvention of restrictive regulations. And these regulations were permanent. In 1590 the crown prohibited trade with the East via Panama and Mexico. As of 1582 direct private trade between Mexico and Peru was forbidden, as well as the navigation of private boats among the American and Eastern colonies. Spain's obsession with blocking Chinese goods crossing the Pacific via the Philippines bound for Peru moved Spain to try to protect its monopoly with the prohibition of traffic between the two coasts in 1579. In 1634, almost a century after meeting with illegal forces breaking up the monopoly everywhere, the crown prohibited all trade among the American colonies. Toward the end of the sixteenth century Peruvian mercury was sought after by the viceroyality of New Spain (Mexico) for the amalgamation of metals. But the Andalusian monopolists, in collusion with those in power, boycotted this trade right from the beginning. Once confined to Peru, the trade was placed, like everything else, in the hands of a chosen few.

The economic system blocked the creation of a really dynamic and all-encompassing Peruvian market. It was not only stifled by a small and enriched group of monopolies; it was also oriented almost exclusively to export. In exchange the colonies received what they needed filtered through a small commercial elite, who arbitrarily set prices. Apart from the participation of a certain number of Indians in commercial activities around work centers—mines and *haciendas*—supplying the local community, the majority of the population had no access to the market as such. The colonial market was minimal and was weighed down by the double power of restrictive legislation and a monopolist elite. The absence of a vast market in the interior of Peru is the major cause of the social disintegration that the republic inherited. The nonprivileged

Peruvian was just one more statistic in the work-force registers (at that point he was generally hired, or badly hired). Learning to cheat the law and trick the monopoly, twisting and winding amid the complications of colonial legality, many Peruvians as well as Spanish authorities discovered that illegality was the only way to gain access to a market, although the underground market differed greatly from the other one protected by law and authority. It was the functionary and not the consumer and the producer who decided the economic life of Peruvians. Thanks to Spain, the culture of the functionary, which the Incas had established in Peru, took on immense proportions. Thus, the state slowly became fiction. The institutions became a vague reference with no authority or legitimacy, despite a rhetorical cult of formal legality and a profusion of rules and regulations that might indicate the contrary. The buying of public posts, where not only Spaniards were involved, became common. As we shall see, this is a reality that the republic extended, turning the underground economy developing on the edge of legality into the only form of survival of the great mass of Peruvians, and public posts into profitable business.

Because of all this there emerged a fractured and disintegrated society with vast differences resulting more from privilege than capacity and even from race in a society so stratified that it resembled those *andenes* or footpaths in Peru's sierra mountains that seem like stairs. Today's civilian society is the remote offspring of that society. The transfer of the population to work in the mines (the *mita*) or in the *obraje* dislocated the native peoples. It did not do away with the community, but it did bring about a social trauma among the indigenous institutions. Without a doubt, it was a system of exploitation. In time, forced labor became paid labor. In the eighteenth century we see the greater part of silver mining done by people working voluntarily for salaries. There was also a salary system in the *obrajes*. But both forms of labor coexisted for some time in the *haciendas*. The only Indians with privileges were those related to the ruling cast in the time of the Incas, and a number of *curacas*. A relationship with political power was the only way of rising in society. And this was restricted to a tiny minority that moved to the main cities and had dealings with the Spanish elite. Of course these people never enjoyed the same rights as the latter. But the system did introduce a differentiation between the native elite and the masses of Peruvians suffering discrimination. There was also a small group, called *yanakunas*, who abandoned the communities and went permanently in the service of the Spaniards at the *haciendas*. These people would not be privileged; but neither would they suffer the hardships of the majority of the population.

The state created a corporate system with a society compartmentalized according to one's function. And this function was to a large extent determined by one's race and origin. The blacks, arriving with the colony, worked on the *haciendas* of the coast and served important families there. The majority of the Indians remained in the interior as laborers. But with the economic recession of the eighteenth century, large numbers of Indians migrated to the cities to become members of guilds or to assist the clergy. In order to use this labor and control the population the Spaniards also took advantage of such native institutions as the *mita*, the *curaca*, the peasant community, and tribute. The mestizos were also discriminated against, but to a lesser extent. For example, they did not have to pay the tribute exacted from the Indians. Individuals resulting from the cross between mestizos and Indians (the Peruvian *cholo*) were forced to pay the tribute, but were not forced to participate in the *mita*.

Curiously, the *mestizo* population, a major characteristic of Spanish colonialism—in contrast, for example, with English colonialism—gave us nothing less than Diego de Almagro, the second Spanish ruler of Peru, the son of a Panamanian Indian woman. But in the eyes of the colony the phenomenon was considered a social stigma. What we call *criollos* were the offspring of Spaniards born in the Americas, and later the moving force behind independence. They also suffered the consequences of colonial domination; they could benefit from their origins in comparison to Indians and mestizos, but for a long time the doors to political power were closed to them. They could not participate in the administration and only became important members of Peruvian society around the eighteenth century. Finally there was the dominant cast made up of "peninsular" Spaniards. This was the political, social, and economic right arm of the metropolis.

And so Peruvian society gradually became, between the sixteenth and nineteenth centuries, a *criollo-mestizo*-Indian-black hybrid society. (The coming of several dozens of Asian slaves along with smuggled goods between the Philippines and Peru in the sixteenth century began a small and nonvoluntary flow of Asians across the Pacific).[1] But one of the great misfortunes of the colonial experience is the fact that miscegenation was insufficient. Miscegenation in Spanish colonies, which differed radically from English colonization, was a key element of that historical phase. It encompassed race as well as religion. This explains, for example, the emergence of the Lord of Miracles in Peru (*El Señor de los Milagros*) and the Virgin of Guadalupe in Mexico, who in the sixteenth century imprinted herself on Diego's Indian mantle and turned dark and Latin American.

Although statistically miscegenation seems huge, the truth is that the purely indigenous half of Peruvian society has lived together up until now with another half divided between a mestizo majority and a *criollo* minority, which, owing to the nature of our institutions, so poorly bent on integration and so undemocratic, have become compartmentalized. The republic did not correct the social stratification of the colony, because the essence of the problem is not really racial but institutional. The fact that the colony failed to promote a large market in which all citizens of any race could participate with equal rights is the main cause of the weakness of our miscegenation. Our racial admixture was not accompanied by an institutional, political, economic, and social admixture. Later on, the republic, incapable of making radical changes in state-society relationships inherited from the colony (despite the pretty words of our constitutions), brought us to our present state. That colonial society produced, for example, the rebellion of Túpac Amaru in the eighteenth century with all its antiwhite hatred. It was therefore opposed by whites and by a small elite of local *caciques* who had vested interests in the system.

Several of the colonial characteristics I have mentioned above varied somewhat with the Bourbon reforms in the eighteenth century when they replaced the Hapsburgs. On dividing the viceroyality into intendances (*intendencias*), the foundations were laid for the division of the territory into nations. The Bourbon era brought on the beginnings of the decay of the *hacienda* and the growth of trade. It eased the rise of a commercial bourgeoisie greater than under the former regime thanks to liberalization, and it fostered an easier religious morale. It opened more doors to power for the *criollo*; and this created the foundations of stronger pro-independence sentiments among a class that began to feel that Spain was an intruder and that there was a "Peruvian consciousness." But at the same time the Bourbons brought in an enlightened despotism they had learned from the French. There was more centralization. There was an obsession with spying on the colonizers and a more rigid control over what was happening beyond the seas. In essence, these changes did not alter relationships between the state and society in the colonies. They had a certain modernizing repercussion among the *criollo* elite, which took on ideas imported from France and England. There thrived, also, a small commercial bourgeoisie. But the power structure remained more or less intact. However, there was one crucial difference: a weakening of the "peninsulars" (peninsular Spaniards) in the face of the growing strength of the *criollos* who would soon be the rulers of Peru in the republican period.

The colonial state and society inheritance was not essentially modified under republican rule in the last century. The great historical excuses blaming the colonial heritage for republican failures fall apart faced with clear evidence that the very republic, led by Peruvians, perpetuated and worsened the essential vices of the system. The state continued to be centralist, interventionist, corrupt, suffocating, discriminating, elitist, and authoritarian. We can point out, for example, that colonial legislation was in effect in Peru until 1852, several decades after independence. The dictatorial governments continued to change, but they did nothing other than modify the nomenclature of power instead of its structure. The society remained fragmented, stratified, static, parasitic, and suffering all-pervading discrimination. The sense of that "Peruvian nation," which the *criollos* made theirs on the birth of the republic, was not part of the thinking of the majority of the sons and daughters of the nation. Although in the case of people like Simón Bolívar, the great figure of Latin American independence, the *criollo* idea of nationhood meant an ethnically plural society, it is shocking to see that the indigenous community was not officially recognized as such in Peru until the 1980 Constitution.

The president, the Supreme Court, the prefects, and the municipalities replaced the viceroys, the courts, the intendances, and the councils. Centralism and nationalism finished off such federal efforts as the Peru-Bolivia Confederation of 1836. An appetite for power on the part of military cliques and their civilian favorites blocked such attempts at modernization as that of Manuel Vidaurre. He wanted to invert the military/civilian hierarchy in government affairs, promote religious tolerance with a substantial reduction in the power of the clergy, as well as abolish colonial tributes. Liberal gains were few and far between. Ramón Castilla, for example, did manage some reforms; but he could not essentially modify the structure of the state regarding its function in the lives of Peruvian citizens. Attempts to decentralize through departmental and municipal juntas did not give the different and distant regions of the country more power. They became simply an extension of central power, which weakened attempts by the provinces to achieve autonomous existence.

Civilian participation in Peruvian politics burst onto the scene in the final years of the century. But it became a superposition of civilian organizations on the economic and social structure consolidated by the republican era. The dominant note was the lack of access to the capitalist market (and its sine qua non condition, property) of the majority of Peruvians. So this political participation became an expression of the vices in society and not an instrument of authentic civilian partaking in the nation's affairs. Such a participation did not come until the beginning of the twentieth century when mass movements erupted onto the scene during the end of the Leguía dictatorship. But even then participation was limited by an essential feature of the republic: the absence of a large middle class.

The republic only managed, with a certain commercial liberalization, to obtain English foreign capital—and later on U.S. capital—to compensate for a lack of capital on the part of the *criollos* and create a certain dynamism in the system itself. So the English came to control trade in sugar, cotton, and metals within regulations laid down by the Peruvian government. But the *entreguismo* (sell out)of which the republic is often accused did not exist. The rules of the game were made by the Peruvian government; and we have to thank these foreigners for coming and breathing a bit of life into an economy that was not very diversified and was lacking capital. The tragedy is that the system, which remained untouched, blocked the formation of a Peruvian bourgeoisie. This meant that civilians with some training, instead of creating wealth, gave themselves over to sniffing about in the little political world where they could not even participate fully thanks to the iron hand of the military cast. The pattern of the possession of wealth and of the means of production remained intact. A small group had taken over the properties of the church, the government, and the municipalities. The Peruvian economy was basically pre-industrial and based on agriculture. *Latifundios* (landed estates) and mining predominated, depending on very poorly paid Indian labor. Along the coast, the *haciendas* used the same cheap labor, but the workers were normally not Indians. They were mainly blacks; and later there were *coolies* from China. The fact that Peru was fortunate enough to find buyers for its agricultural production did not modify the structures of a system that only served to enrich a small and exclusive group of owners who did not diversify the economy so that others might have access to the sources of wealth.

In the middle of the century Peru was hit by a stroke of luck, stumbling upon a new source of wealth: *guano*. The fertilizing properties from this substance, from the 1940s up until the war with Chile (1879), gave Peru's rentier economy a powerful thrust ahead. European farmers became ongoing buyers of this fertilizer. The consignment system prevailed until in 1868 the Dreyfus house was sold outright a considerable quantity of *guano* to be traded as it wished. It is not fair, either, to attack the republic that emerged in the nineteenth century for allowing the participation of foreign capital in the exploitation of guano. Peru took back an average of 60 percent of the benefits of this income, something perfectly acceptable for a country that lacked its own capital necessary for production. The disastrous consequences of the *guano* business can be blamed only on Peruvians. In the first place, there was the government monopoly via a system of consignment, which at several points saw the participation of Peruvian as well as foreign businessmen. In the second place, the squandering of money blocked the creation in Peru of a diversified economy and a modern infrastructure with the resources obtained. It gave birth to a cult of public spending from which we still suffer today; and it ended by putting Peru in debt up to its neck. The first great culprit regarding Peru's debt was Nicolás de Piérola, the mythical republican leader of the second half of the nineteenth century. From this collusion between a small mafia of capitalists and a monopolistic state there came, perfected and expanded, the same mercantilist practices originating with the colony and that were to become Peru's endemic trait.

In the 1920s the dictatorship of Augusto Leguía pushed the mercantilist economy ahead. That is, he favored a collusion between a privileged plutocracy and a discriminating state. But he also carried this pattern to the area of Peru's emerging industry. The attempts of men like Nicolás Piérola to unblock the Peruvian economy were left behind, as we have seen above. What we inherited in this century from men like him was not the struggle against the unjust privilege of the powerful, but a deformed vision of this fight, an envy of success and a hatred of wealth. Something very damaging for a country that wants to become prosperous is mistrust of wealth and a combat against richness and the rich. One of the great sources of confusion in the nineteenth century has been seeing the causes of Peruvian misery in the rich man or the foreigner and not in the system itself.

So the civilian society in Peru formed by the republic continued to suffer from the same impediments working against integration, economic miscegenation, mobility, and the creation of a bourgeoisie, that is, a middle class, which might be the pillars of a modern Peru. The natives continued working hard for a pittance in the sierra. On the coast blacks and Chinese *coolies* served propertied families, while the mestizos played an intermediate role as tools of powerful elements in watching over the lowest ranks in Peruvian society, the Indians. In the *haciendas* of the sierra the *criollos* put the mestizos in charge of things. The mestizos functioned as an intermediate class. They were a group with no personal economic identity, a mere reflection of a society fragmented by a social hierarchy that placed the *criollos* at the top of the pyramid and forced the Indians to the bottom.

So, given this state of things, we should not be surprised to see the strong emergence in Peruvian politics of socialism via the APRA party of Haya de la Torre and the Socialist party of Mariátegui. This meant that the Peruvian middle class had finally become part of society. But once again, an opportunity was lost. The Leguía government promoted a mercantilist capitalism and a growth of the state. It forced the middle class to take refuge in bureaucracy instead of operating in its natural habitat: the creation of wealth. APRA gathered an alliance of the middle and working classes emerging in a Peru that was slowly industrializing within the system. Socialism, a minority force, also had the support of the latter. Denouncing the system, many Peruvians identified with the socialist message. It was the first great mobilization in Peru after centuries of wrong turns by the colony and the republic.

A civil movement with a truly liberal orientation was snowed under by the great division between pro-APRA and anti-APRA forces. This counterpoint between a failed system on the defensive and remedies that confused the causes of the failure, and proposed new forms guaranteed to sink the country further into misery blocked an opening in the political firmament that might have provided a space for change and renovating ideas as apart from the colonial and republican inheritance as the socialist option.

There was a crisis in the system and in the 1970s Velasco Alvarado brought in a socialism that Haya de la Torre had not been allowed to establish half a century before, with all the vile consequences mentioned above. APRA should have governed in Peru in the 1930s and the 1940s, and we would have saved a number of lost decades. In the first place, the socialist adventure of Alan García's democratic government in the 1980s would have been almost inconceivable without the official veto lasting decades against his party and its ideas, which froze both in a vision of the past imbued with overall failure.

To the earlier evils of the republic Velasco added statism; he expropriated national and foreign firms right and left (there was also a tradition of this in Peru with Piérola's expropriations of domestic capitalists in the last century). Velasco created over 200 public enterprises, fomented hatred of economic success, and, on the coast and in the sierra, he replaced the *haciendas* with the state cooperatives that caused so much frustration in the Peruvian countryside and that later offered fertile ground for the development of *Sendero Luminoso*. He upset private mercantilism only to replace it with state control, in line with a Peruvian tradition of replacing certain evils with worse ones that never finished off what they wanted to replace, but creating a useless hybrid of old and new evils.

In the 1950s and the 1960s the growth of industry and of services led to the emergence of many professionals, technicians, and educators. This brought about the creation of such political parties as the Popular Action party and the Christian Democrats, along with its breakaway groups, the Popular Christian party, which marks the contemporary stage, together with APRA and Marxism. The Velasco experiment frustrated that generation, crushing it and forcing it to live painfully inside the system. It also killed off the efforts of private capitalism that, although subjected to the old system, had brought some wealth to Peru. The prosperous fishing industry is one example. Like always throughout our history, the axe lopped off the best heads as soon as they were raised. The democracy that returned in 1980 gave more strength to the mercantilist system, and it did not touch the state. The sum of these experiences goes a long way toward explaining today's Peru.

But this Peru cannot be understood without taking into account the social revolution organized spontaneously by Peruvians in recent decades, which has been called the "informal economy." In the most recent stage of our republic Peruvian civil society has carried out the revolution the state refused to promote. The phenomenon is based on the massive migration of Indians and mestizos from the country to the city, from the province to the capital. This began in the times of Manuel Odría in the 1950s and has increased sharply in more recent years. The consequence is an overflow of the cities and the institutions operating there. Cast aside for so long by the state, Peruvians have decided to throw their weight against it. They surround it from the marginal belt, neighborhoods grown on the outskirts of the capital, and have begun to create popular institutions substituting the official ones. There is a parallel legality and a consuetudinary law within which these Peruvians create wealth and contribute in this way to a stumbling nation.

No one is consciously organizing this revolution. It is spontaneous, the sum of individual decisions in the daily lives of people with similar problems. The result is an underground economy, an economy in the shadows. But it is not something Peru has invented. Many peoples throughout history have opted for the creation of wealth apart from the law when legal systems, political realities, and social restrictions impeded the free access of a population emerging in the cities to the sources of wealth. Medieval and Renaissance Europe itself, which gave birth to the Latin American colonies, was a world with a variety of economic activities taking place apart from the official institutions. What distinguishes contemporary Peru is the magnitude of the phenomenon, far superior to any other economy in Latin America. The world on the perimeter (although this word is not exactly correct when we are speaking of such a vast population) of the capital and other cities is an example of market economy and private enterprise in Peru that has given the defenders of freedom a great deal of hope and arms to beat back socialism, mercantilism and the republican state.

Above all, the world of immigrants moving from the country to the city is the expression of an economic reality: the impossibility of creating wealth in their places of origin. The phenomenon of industrialization has created a movement of the population to the cities in many parts of the world. In the case of Peru, it was more the smothering of the countryside and the decadence of provincial towns, and not industrialization, that uprooted millions of Indians and mestizos from their places of origin.

Political violence in the last decade has given this movement an incredible impact. The result of the process is that the population of the city of Lima has grown from 700,000 inhabitants in 1940 to over 7 million in the early 1990s. The urban growth is at some 1,200 percent. The cities have seen their surroundings blown to pieces and transformed, while there is a limited capacity of services and employment opportunities preventing them from welcoming the new citizens. The result has been a spontaneous economy, as always happens in the market, developing on the fringes but without the protection and guarantees of a state of law, with all the limitations, and there are many, emerging from this. And so while these Peruvians invented such forms of creating wealth as ambulatory streetselling, construction, transport and light industry, there emerged a citizens' code of conduct able to offer a minimum of legal frameworks for this world. The result is what such researchers as Enrique Gersi and Hernando de Soto have called "extra-legal regulations" and "consuetudinary law".[2] This is but the Peruvian version of experiences like common law adopted by official British institutions born from the common dealings of the people. All official institutions have received some form of popular response.

The Catholic church, for example, an institution that in our country has been linked with the power structure for so many centuries, has had to face the emergence of a multitude of Protestant groups. This came out very clearly in the electoral process of 1990 where there was a great deal of tension between the Catholic bishops and the Fujimori advisers, which caused the archbishop of Lima to call a procession honoring the *Señor de los Milagros* in May instead of the traditional date in October. The Catholic church is only one of Peru's official institutions that has been overwhelmed by the response of the poor. The most important, of course, is the law itself. It is massively ignored in everyday routine, but with no implications of criminality. Since in Peru the official institutions have drawn farther and farther away from daily life, there has been no osmosis between the two worlds of legality and daily life. The people have made good Henry David Thoreau's idea, expressed in his essay "Civil Disobedience," that "it is not desirable to cultivate a respect for the law, so much as for the right." What has resulted is a divorce that has brought about more and more violent confrontations and a certain anarchy in everyday life. The underground economy has attenuated this crisis to a considerable extent since, without its volume, the solutions proposed by *Sendero Luminoso* would have taken hold more quickly and more widely. The inhabitants of shantytowns make up one-half of the country's economically active population. They account for 40 percent of total production. In areas such as transport, for example, they provide 90 percent of the services. This means that without them Lima would be immobilized. There has also been a spontaneous freeing up of the system in the Peruvian countryside. The peasants themselves continue to parcel out (that is, privatize) state cooperatives created under Velasco and not officially broken up under democracy. This illegal privatizing in the country amounts to over 60 percent of cultivated lands. It is the agrarian reflection of the popular revolution taking place in the cities. This underground economy is necessarily limited. As such its contribution, which has been decisive in the subsistence of the migratory population, disallowing a general civil war from breaking out, is still not enough. The indispensable complement is precisely an adaptation of Peruvian institutions inherited from colonialism and republicanism to this new reality in order to close the gap separating the two aspects of Peruvian life and dissolve the real and potential violence emanating from the rupture.

Throughout the 1980s a number of Peruvians fought a solitary battle in an attempt to convince the power structure as well as the Peruvians from the underground economy, to open its eyes to reality. One of the most shocking paradoxes of our political life has been that in all these years the inhabitants in question have come out in favor of political options that have nothing to do with their own interests as expressed in their economic revolution. They represent free enterprise; but they were the first to back the left and APRA, which never understood that informal economy was not the problem but the solution to the Peruvian crisis and that there must be a modernization of institutions within a vast state reform based on freedom. What these inhabitants represented in daily life was precisely civil society's response to the state.

This lack of communication between the parties and civil society, between state and citizens, created a situation that was more and more problematic. Eighty percent of our population is unemployed or underemployed. One-half lives in a condition of poverty. A third of Peruvian children are undernourished, and one out of four Peruvians receives aid from international institutions like AID, EEC, and others. The informal economy is not a paradise: it is merely a mechanism of survival for desperate human beings. Its contribution to Peru has been providential. But in a climate of economic collapse produced by mistaken policies, civilian and military ideological violence, a lack of confidence in institutions, laws, and authorities, and a psychological smothering caused by the monumental weight of the state and its bureaucracy, the economy of the poor is still an economy of the poor.

It is impossible to understand this process without grasping the experiences of our past, which I have tried to outline. The republic of Peru has been full of revolutions changing things for the worse, solutions that made problems even graver, changes that meant continuity. But it is possible to discover, under the swerving of successive governments, democratic or dictatorial, a more or less direct route pointing toward bureaucracy, regulations, state control, and mercantilism. And there is one constant lesson: the more the legislation, the greater the poverty.

Among the 26,000 laws promulgated since the beginning of the century, a third appeared under the Velasco dictatorship. And since that time the average economic output rate has fallen by 1.6 percent. In recent times the great promulgators of norms and laws regulating Peruvians' lives have not been the parliamentarians, but the ministers and their subordinates. The Peruvian state has come to employ a 1.5 million people, nearly all of them family heads. This means that a third of the nation is supported by the public budget. And each bureaucratic institution has become a hotbed for specific regulations in social and economic life. Peru is one of the most flagrant cases in the so-called Third World of what Friedrich A. von Hayek describes as the great confusion between law and command,[3] the displacement of common law by positive law and of private law by public law. What has been understood as law during colonial and republican times in Peru were really specific rules designed to benefit or harm select groups of people. This custom has placed the law in the hands of the discretional power of the authorities, perfectly apart from the uses and customs of civil society. It is the latter that in principle should dictate norms of conduct (common law), limiting the intervention of power to the verdict of a judge in cases of conflicts that cannot be solved. What has happened in Peru in recent times is the perfection and increase in the dangerous tradition that makes power the arbitrary source of laws instead of the guarantor of general, abstract, and preferably unwritten norms within which the people could develop freely.

In some cases this process has been carried out with good intentions. Nonetheless, it has turned thousands of obscure bureaucrats into legislators. The result has been a smothering of civil society and the impossibility of creating wealth. The economy of the poor is the response to this lack of balance in relations between authority and society, with the emergence of an active private life regulated by spontaneous law.

Today's civil society suffers from a double inheritance: that of the social fractures appearing in the country's different historical stages; and that of the permanence in our state of all those vices that blocked the formation of a broad democratic culture allowing, through a competitive market, for the integration of those millions of Peruvians who in recent decades have gotten an education and moved to urban centers. Given this frustration, it is not difficult to understand the racial, social, and political violence that was just under the surface for many years and that emerged as a prominent characteristic of contemporary Peru at the end of the 1980s and the dawn of the 1990s. From the 1990 electoral campaign up until now political confrontation has been invariably accompanied by a verbal (and physical) violence loaded with racial, nationalist, or simply class hatred.

One of the great challenges facing my father in the 1990 electoral campaign was communicating with the diverse elements making up Peru's cultural mosaic, from the Amazon communities to the *criollo* minority, because the nonintegrated evolution of these different communities means that a Peruvian who takes up politics must meet the difficulty of speaking to all of them at once. If the diagnosis of the crisis points to a divorce between he who rules and the citizen, the solution calls for (prior to the application of policies restoring confidence between power and society) a communication between the two parties established on the same wavelength. This is the only way the State can gain the necessary popular confidence to carry out these difficult reforms, a definite source of conflict with so many vested interests, whose final result might be a remaking of the role of the institutions.

We were quite conscious of the need to find a language that would offer an electoral victory emerging from a convinced and lucid vote. One of the great frustrations of that fleeting political experience was to discover that in Peru there is also a separation between the deep instincts of the society and its conscious vision when it is time to express a political preference. Those same men who in their daily lives embodied the policies that we obsessively put forward in the streets and the plazas of the country rejected outright a radical change and a serious transformation. It was as though this modus vivendi of the economy of the poor was something preferable to achieving real prosperity. In the final analysis it was a deeply conformist option in favor of the status quo in a country where the status quo offered misery everywhere. And behind this there was a refusal to believe, a rejection of hope. At times one thought pessimistically that a nihilist mentality had overtaken Peruvians after so many years of shattered dreams, so many false promises, so many failures, and the weight of resentment that these painful experiences had built up in the national spirit.

I had a direct encounter with this reality the morning I went to the Hotel Crillón in downtown Lima with my father to congratulate Alberto Fujimori on his electoral triumph. At the Fujimori campaign headquarters there was an absence of the throngs that normally come out to celebrate the victory of their candidate. A few supporters milled about shouting racist slogans; but there was not even a hint of the festive and crowded atmosphere associated with an electoral triumph, especially one so unexpected and after such a hard battle.

The vote seemed more out of revenge than enthusiasm. The victory celebration was not a popular outpouring but a solitary and quiet rumination, almost filled with shame. It was a revenge which, as the initial enthusiasm with the dictatorship brought out, reached its peak on the day of the coup d'état. Japanese *Bushido*, which is the ascetic moral code of the Samurais, calls for suicide as a form of expiation. Among the subjects of the Peruvian-Japanese Alberto Fujimori, political suicide has the air of vengeance.

In this kind of scene, the top priority is communication. Communication is the bridge that must be crossed by the institutions in their voyage to the heart of society. We made such an effort to communicate in the 1990 campaign, to the point of saturation. We understood that, before applying specific policies, it would be necessary to establish an understanding, a common language between the official country and the society in general, and work out within the popular imagination a logical relationship between the causes of the people's suffering and the Peruvian state against which we struck out so often. We hoped that our solutions which on the surface seemed like sacrifices would be seen as a natural consequence of the state of things and as the only way out. It was a challenge to speak simultaneously with Peruvians who used different languages—Spanish, Quechua, Aymara, and Amazon dialects—among themselves and lived in different cultural stages: antiquity, the Middle Ages, and modern times. The key seemed to be bringing in an intellectual dimension with ideas via formulas not too sophisticated but certainly above low-passionate politics and in making a great effort to replace populist demagogy and electoralist lies with a strong dose of sincerity. The result was a serious lack of communication. It was as though we had come too late. The Democratic Front did get a lot of votes in many of the shantytowns, 50,000 in San Juan de Lurigancho with 350,000 inhabitants and almost 44 percent in all of Lima, which has a third of the country's population. We also did well in many provinces (almost 30 percent in Cuzco and Junín in the Andes). But the lack of confidence in politicians, the incredulity, and in many cases the resentment were too strong to render our attempts at communication successful.

A short-lived coming together of interests between the poor of Peru and the business class, such as the one brought about by the capture of Abimael Guzmán, does not free the essential causes of this crisis from responsibility: the absence of a commonly accepted ideological language, and, first and foremost, the lack of movement within the official country against its political inheritance. So the general tendency has not changed direction, although there have been minor breaks. At the beginning a dictatorship usually creates a sense of order, an order that is out to replace the democratic anarchy. With time this order becomes an actuality with no relationship to the real structure of things. It becomes a temporary freezing of time.

Chiang Kai-Chek's repression of the communists in the wake of his victory over the military in the north of China seemed to be an establishment of order. The same happened with the foreign invading forces in Vietnam, against which Ho Chi Min rose up, and with the Cambodia of Lon Nol. All these experiences brought on worse evils. It is not the abrupt taking of power by *Sendero Luminoso* that might result from the prolongation of dictatorship in Peru. But this perpetuation of authoritarianism can indeed cause in time a metastasis of the tumor to the social body. The Peruvian government, an heir to decades of authoritarian failure, will, in time, worsen the inability of Peruvian society to integrate and crystallize a broad and solid middle class, and form relationships of respect and communication with the institutions that rule its life. This inability, the consequences of which in the fast-moving and competitive world of today are infinitely more serious than in the past, is the major ally of *Sendero* and other forms of subversion that might emerge.

Thus, there are certain points to be made. If the success in the capture of Guzmán is not accompanied by a return to democracy in the country, subversion and violence will survive this hard blow, because the reasons for its existence will continue. These reasons are only explained in part by the petite-bourgeoisie mentality of certain déclassé individuals taking refuge in the Marxist-Leninist-Maoist catechism. They are explained as well by a historical fracturing of the society to which the Peruvian state contributed from its very existence. The radical solution lies not in repeating past experiences with certain fashionable or contemporary touches. It lies in a political break with that past, which will give society the means of defense—such as property, business, legality—against the real enemy. The greater part of Peru needs this, which is why, without knowing a single word of Marxism, many Peruvians contribute to the drunken violence of *Sendero Luminoso*. In a society with no belief in its institutions it is not always easy to establish the border line between those who break the law peacefully and those who do it violently.

There is a social virus that in the future could take on new forms differing from this peculiarity called *Sendero*. They would be an embodiment of those same things essential to *Sendero*: the imposition of an ideology of death on the violent surface of Peruvian society; a culture of resentment among a population with reasons for hate; a disdain for legality among men and women who earn their livings apart from it; a racist conviction among the heirs of a long-standing discrimination; and class struggle in a world where the word capitalism has never meant, as it means in civilized societies, a democratic access to the sources of wealth, but the privileged use of these tools by a few.

This permanent danger is only encouraged by the nature of the de facto regime in Peru, which entails more of the same, despite the fact that many Peruvians see it, according to official propaganda, as a break with the past. It continues along the lines of the great institutional and social imbalance characterizing our pre-Columbian, our colonial, and our republican life, that has brought us to our present state. It revives these mirages of change that have appeared suddenly in our history every time a new regime imposed by force announces a new and different era. In today's Peru the observation of Aristotle is more valid than ever: "The truth of things is not in actual appearances, but in the sense of their tendencies."

Notes

1. Fernando Iwasaki Cauti, *Extremo oriente y Perú en el siglo XVI* (Madrid: MAPFRE, 1992).
2. Hernando de Soto and Enrique Ghersi, *El Otro Sendero* (*The Other Path*) (Lima: El Barranco, 1986).
3. Friedrich A. von Hayek, *Law, Legislation and Liberty* (Chicago: University of Chicago Press, 1973-79).

4

Peru and the New World Order

The collapse of Peruvian democracy came at a cutoff point in Latin American history. The coup d'état was the offspring of Peruvian and Latin American political traditions. It exploded paradoxically just when the American continent was seeing a drawing away from the major constants of our republican political life, in all its ramifications. In domestic politics there is the upsurge of a broad-based democracy with strong popular roots, differing from previous democratic experiences, which were weak-kneed and limited in scope. Regarding the economy, there is a rejection of state authority and a new value placed on the principles of freedom and market realities. Concerning foreign policy, we witness a discovery of the Western model and re-evaluation of its champion, the United States, a country with which the Latin American democracies are quickly finding a great deal in common.

Peru is not swimming against the current, at least politically, of this continental wave by mere chance. Quite the contrary. Peru is the reflection of a threat underlying the surface and appearance of things in several of the Latin American democracies that give the impression today of leaping toward modernity. All of these democracies should contemplate themselves in this way, because the same destiny awaits them if they cannot manage to achieve the objectives they have set before there is a devastating outbreak of popular impatience.

Precisely some of that is what we saw in Venezuela in February 1992 when a regiment of paratroopers from Maracay led a group of military men in an attempt to bring down President Carlos Andrés Pérez. This sparked off a sort of national antidemocratic euphoria that turned persons like Lieutenant-Colonel Chávez into heroes. And it is what we have seen in the four coup attempts between 1987 and 1990 in Argentina during the

Alfonsín and Menem governments. They showed that the military *carapintadas*, while they were not overwhelmingly popular among the masses, do enjoy a certain prestige among their colleagues. This explains why names like Aldo Rico and Mohammed Alí Seineldín suddenly became famous. The coup against democratic president Jean-Bertrand Aristide in Haiti in September 1991 is admittedly different from the above cases regarding its very specific characteristics. It destroyed the first democratic regime since the black cimarron uprisings brought independence to the republic in 1804. But it is still part of an antidemocratic presence that threatens weak civilian governments throughout the continent. And the coup by President Serrano in Guatemala in May 1993 was not initially responded to by the people; only a few journalists, politicians, retired generals, and the attorney general voiced their opposition, and, encouraged by international support, cracks developed within the military and made it impossible for Serrano to continue in power.

The old dictatorial tendencies have been successful only in Peru and Haiti; elsewhere, they are a daunting threat. But there is still the impression that we are living in a new historical era. A look at this reality is worthwhile, because it is in the face of it that we must measure the Peruvian case. The fall of democracy here hits hard at the consciousness of the whole continent and makes it wonder: can we have in the near future continental mechanisms to preserve these recent achievements and prevent the enemies of democracy from crashing it before it has come of age?

In Central America between the end of the 1970s and the beginning of the 1990s, the "domino effect" toppled the dictatorships in Honduras, Guatemala, El Salvador and Panama (the last with the help of winds from the north). In South America, we had, similarly, the end of dictatorships in Peru, Brazil, Argentina, Uruguay, Bolivia, Paraguay, Guyana, and, for several days, Surinam. There were the two sides of the coin in this process, each one expressing a historical phenomenon. The first is the defeat of a political model—the military *caudillo* system—which had ruled Latin American republican life on and off and was responsible for three great evils: violence, the absence of respectable and lasting civilian institutions, and populism. The second side of the coin is different only in appearance: a farewell to revolution. Twenty-five years ago General Barrientos finished off the legendary Ché Guevara, the Rousseauistic good savage. The military/revolutionary dichotomy confronted Latin American societies. The military regimes won in Argentina, Uruguay, and Chile; but they were defeated in Cuba and Nicaragua by the revolutionaries. Only Venezuela finished the latter off the civilian way, with the government of Rómulo Betancourt, which helped prop up the country's democracy. In Peru Fernando Belaunde sent military men to the mountains to quell the guerrilla movement in the 1960s. Their mission completed, they then proceeded to conquer democracy. In El Salvador there seemed to be a military standoff.

It is clear today that this was a mistaken choice for Latin America. Both the military dictators and the revolutionaries were defeated. But they were, in the final analysis, an expression of the same evil. They bathed the streets and jungles of the Americas with blood; and they also sunk their countries into economic misery (except for the special case of the Chilean dictatorship, which was more competent than its peers regarding economic policy). Civilian governments emerging from more or less honest elections replaced the two types of dictator, although there are the exceptional cases of Cuba and Mexico. Despite the later exceptions of Peru and Haiti (and the much forgotten Surinam), democratic regimes are common currency in Latin America. They are backed by the majority of citizens, regardless of how they feel about their respective governments. Conditions are given for the creation of a civil, institutional life of a permanent nature.

This Latin American democratic wave coincides with the upsurge of the liberal Western culture around the world,[1] which began with the communist debacle started in 1985 and symbolized in a spectacular form by the revolutions of 1989. This, for example, has led Francis Fukuyama to declare the end of Hegelian history.[2] One of the great international questions of our times is how to secure the permanence of these liberal and democratic achievements, how to convert this fashion into a worldwide constant. Amid the flood of historical developments in recent times, we heard rumors of a "new world order." The words, which seem to sum up today's circumstances, were heard in every corner of the planet, including Latin America. We as well, with our moves toward democracy, seemed to deserve our own place in the sun in this new world order. When President Bush talked about "the end of the Dictator" we identified immediately, even though the specific and immediate reference was to the Middle East. This climate of international democratic expansion coincided with the growth of large economic blocks in Europe, Asia, and North America. When President Bush launched his Initiative of the Americas on 27 June 1990 we were being invited de facto to take a vanguard position on the new universal political-economic map. We could not ask for a greater expression of hospitality. The United States was the only superpower still alive, and to a certain extent the guarantor of this new world order. It was offering to end those secular hemispheric confrontations and make the south of the continent an important piece in the world liberal-democratic machinery.

Today the reasons for such optimism are more or less still valid and the virtues contained in that announcement are still alive. But the mechanisms for putting things into effect have not been created anywhere. The world is still divided between a democratic renaissance and the confrontation of economic blocks; and the dictatorial exceptions are still too numerous and serious to think that "the end of the dictator" is no more than a coincidence. That coincidence must yet be turned into a permanent feature for all humanity.

In Latin America, for example, the case of Peru has shown that this new order is still a utopia. Most of Latin America is under democratic rule; but the exceptions are a continental benchmark given the recent coup attempts in various countries and, what is even more symptomatic, given the near impossibility of restoring democracy via hemispheric action where it has been rent asunder. Despite strong international pressure, Peru has become a *fait accompli* allowing much of the international community to wash its hands of those affairs. The economic virtues of Mexico have also relaxed efforts to force the *Partido Revolucionario Institucional* (PRI) to become more democratic. Meanwhile, various Latin American countries refuse to cooperate with Washington's efforts to end the Castro dictatorship. The case of Peru is worse. Despite certain initial efforts, the United States as well as the other Latin American countries, without actively collaborating with it, stopped mobilizing against the dictatorship.

So reality has shown, sooner than we thought, that the democratic euphoria was premature. A small group of Haitian or Peruvian military men have been able, despite the spectacular internationalization of contemporary life, to ensnare themselves into isolated dictatorships, successfully defying outside pressure. There is something worse. These spurious governments have brought out the lack of will on the part of the

South American continent to take a strong stand in favor of democracy with something more than telephone calls from some officials expressing solidarity with those defending democracy, empty statements for the press and at hemispheric meetings, a temporary suspension of economic aid, and, in the case of Haiti, a trade embargo. The latter was not levied against Peru for God knows what reason. Democracy has no continental mechanism to assure that the challenges to democracy to it are met.

It is clear that it does not have it either in cases of war. As usually happens, democracies, as opposed to dictatorships, are not inclined to wars. Latin America has undergone five wars since the 1826 failure of the Panama Congress, Bolivar's final effort to offer the continent some form of cohesion. Today it is not international wars that show up the absence of a new continental mechanism to confront a lack of stability. There are internal wars: those unleashed by narco-guerrillas and those unleashed by dictators against civilian society. Although they are internal conflicts, their repercussions beyond national boundaries are dangerous. Fujimori is taken on as a model for several who in Venezuela want the fall of the democratic regime, which they associate with state corruption and the impoverishment of the society. And in January 1993, President Violeta Chamorro of Nicaragua, inspired no doubt by Peru, sent troops to close down Congress temporarily and get hold of official records in a move to replace the parliamentary leadership with more docile politicians. And the coup by president Serrando of Guatemala in 1993 was almost an exact repetition of Fujimori's coup.

Under new international conditions the Peruvian crisis became at once a hemispheric affair. This reality was something new for Peru. As opposed to other Latin American countries, especially the Central American ones, whose political crises immediately become the object of complex foreign policy dealings in the region's foreign affairs bodies with a great deal of information in the continental press, Peruvian politics has carried very little weight on the international scene for a decade. This is not the case with the wide issue of drug dealing, of course, and its links with subversion, which for obvious reasons goes beyond our borders and has caught the attention of the United States and the rest of Latin America. But that has not been a specific political crisis at a precise hour and date calling for determined and immediate action, committing a vast network of hemispheric relationships. It was a more or less permanent factor of the foreign policy of neighbors in the region dealt with in the silent seclusion of routine bureaucratic posts, and which only came to the surface when there was some spectacular assassination or a meeting of presidents in Cartagena de Indias, Colombia, or San Antonio, Texas to coordinate antidrug efforts. For the first time in several years, the Peruvian political crisis became just that: a crisis. That is, it became a contingency that forced deadlines on the international community and made countries in the region make immediate decisions with an eye to a direct effect on events ocurring in Peru, whose destabilizing consequences abroad could be very serious.

As in all crises of political contingency, this one had a potential for immediate developments that might make, depending on the course taken, a decisive impact on the future of the country itself and the whole region. Peruvian drug dealing and subversion have become more or less permanent, stable, and routine factors on the political scene. They are very sporadic sources of international panic; but they do not generally penetrate the nervous hallways of current politics, nor do they make large headlines in the international press. Thanks to the constitutional breakup in a nation undergoing problems potentially affecting the region and in a world context that combines the reconquest of democracy with a growing popular rejection of the overall political class, Fujimori's coup became for a moment an international *issue*. It is not always easy to explain international crises. And it is not always for conscious reasons that governments and the mass media suddenly transform specific national events into objects of continental or international concern or interest. In this mysterious meeting point between specific local events and the international community there are certainly factors having nothing to do with the conscious zone of the human psyche. But the fact is that for several days Peru was the center of international attention, not only on the continent, but also in the European Community and Asia, in the latter case because of the special relationship that ties Japan to a Latin American country ruled by a man of Japanese origin. In these days the international community "discovered" that Peru had (apart from *Sendero Luminoso* and drug dealing) a Constitution, a Parliament, a judicial power, political parties, a controller general, a public prosecutor, and many other forms of civil and democratic institutionality despite their partial rotting.

Unaccustomed to being mobilized by political circumstances originating in Peru, the Latin American and North American community gave signs in those days of having been taken by surprise and of not having a global and homogeneous vision of the country's situation. Sensitive only to drug dealing and *Sendero Luminoso*, the community of American nations was not alert to the political crisis within our democratic institutions. It was not well informed concerning how in recent years (especially since Alberto Fujimori's coming to power) these two extralegal factors had conditioned the proper functioning of the country and its institutions, with the erosion of integrity, morale, and authority. The countries in the region were more prepared to confront the Haitian crisis. But the Peruvian case—with more impact beyond its own borders, and more complex in its make-up—was a break in security and stability in the very heart of Latin America. As far as Peru's neighboring countries, any political focus on the Peruvian case could not disregard domestic repercussions, above all because much of the bacteria eating away at the political and social organism in Peru were present there; and the coup propaganda pointed to deficiencies in democracy elsewhere on the continent. Concerning the United States—overwhelmingly the most important maker of foreign policy decisions in the hemisphere—the situation was especially delicate. The crisis came to shake the very foundations of the new relations between Washington, D.C., and the Latin American capitals and put to the test, too quickly and too abrubtly, a cooperation that had not yet healed the old wounds of a passionate and century-old enmity. This is why the Peruvian case has a special meaning from the point of view of international relations in the hemisphere. For both foreign and domestic reasons Peru became a nerve center of the continental political body, a laboratory of the great tensions between civil society and the governing class that shake Latin America and, of course, an insolent challenge to what we had begun prematurely to call a new order.

The sinew of Latin American international life continues to be the United States. Many countries on the continent define their foreign policies vis-à-vis Washington: some in favor and others against. The United States, after so much confrontation with its neighbors south of the Rio Grande (which has also had repercussions in its own domestic political struggle), is aware of this. Its role is decisive in a case like Peru's. The new understanding between the United States and Latin America has had to stand a number of tests: peace negotiations in El Salvador; the coup against Aristide in Haiti; coup attempts in Buenos Aires and

Caracas; the Colombian decision to prohibit the extradition of drug dealers in its new Constitution; the immense de facto power of the *sandinistas* in the Nicaraguan government of Violeta Chamorro; the stubborn Castro dictatorship; and the invasion of Panama. But none of these crises came out of the blue. Central American policy is a constant focus of attention in U.S. government institutions. The extradition or nonextradition of drug dealers is an ongoing issue on the agenda of bilateral negotiations between Washington and Bogota. The military uprising in Argentina was not the first since the country's return to democracy in the last decade. And in Caracas, Carlos Andrés Pérez was able to put down the rebels. But the Peruvian crisis put to the test the new order being worked out by U.S. and Latin American democracy in a more urgent and striking manner precisely because there was something new in it. It was a successful version of antidemocratic threats that had failed elsewhere and the definitive bursting forth of factors that, despite being a serious threat to the country's institutional stability, had seemed to be unable to bring down the democratic edifice and spark such a continental crisis.

To understand and criticize the U.S. and Latin American response we must have a look at the evolution of relationships between the two poles of the region. This is only the most recent chapter in a long historical tale and could be a disheartening preview of hemispheric inability to create a different order where international guarantees could help maintain a Latin American democracy, no matter how shaky, and put it back on its feet if it stumbles.

There was a very strong Anglo Saxon influence in Latin America at the end of eighteenth century and the beginning of the nineteenth. The American colonies opposed the absolutist thrust and the Counter-Reformation spirit of Spain with the liberal values from the English and French revolutions and the rich British trade experience of the time, a feeding source for an empire at its peak. There has not been sufficient analysis of the influence of English masonry among the independence-minded *criollos* in the Americas, but it did exist. Without a doubt, it was England that filled the gap left by the break with Spain. But then the conditions were different, with an absence of the colonial domination that characterized the previous period.

The United States did not stand apart from this new American scenario. U.S. independence had been the precursor of independence to the south and a large part of its values emerged among us and impregnated our political mentality. A lack of stability, precariousness, and fragility were what most characterized early Latin American independence. And the ability of Spain to recover lost ground or the possibility of intervention by her European rivals was not to be underestimated. In the newborn era of independence, this fluid period of transition to continental sovereignty when the liberated territories could still not form defined national entities able to defend themselves, there was the birth of the Monroe Doctrine of 1823. Here the United States inaugurated what today is called the U.S. "zone of influence" in the hemisphere. The Monroe doctrine was an act of U.S. affirmation on the continent, as well as an extrapolation of its earlier liberal revolution to the field of foreign policy. It was evidence of a struggle between a waning power (Europe) and an emerging power (the United States) in an area where for reasons of history and geography the United States would not accept European imperial power. It was U.S. expansionism as much as an anti-European affirmation.

The United States could not have dominated Latin America on the military level then even if it wanted to; and its economic strength was still not enough to overtake England as the great foreign presence in our commercial life. The Monroe Doctrine is seen today as the precursor of U.S. imperialism in Latin America. And although the date can be clearly identified as the point of departure for the "Latin American concern" in Washington, it should be understood more as a chapter in the maturing of a country as an independent entity faced with European imperialists. That very Monroe Doctrine was also directed at the Russians threatening the northern flank via Alaska. There is no doubt, of course, that involved in this incipient foreign policy was a certain hegemonic inclination. But that would gather shape in time, as the rest of the continent showed itself unable to bring about a powerful and stable unity.

Proof of the above is the fact that the United States spent many years looking inward, strengthening its capitalist dynamics and completing its conquest of the West and the South. It was more concerned with domestic issues than what was happening abroad. U.S. expansion did bring about confrontations with Mexico and meant a vast extension of Mexican lands falling into U.S. hands. Enemies of the United States frequently mention the wars taking place between 1846 and 1848 in which Mexico lost so much territory as an antecedent to policies of domination on the

American continent. Such a point of view is unjustified and a product of arbitrary associations made *a posteriori* and not according to a serious analysis of history. Unjust as they were, these conquests do not form part of a map of continental domination. The United States immediately pulled back afterward to a period of somnolence in foreign policy and a stage of isolationism.

The French, who also made imperialist incursions into Mexico in 1864 and 1867, have not been accused of inaugurating a permanent imperialist policy in Latin America. We must see the U.S. incursion in Mexican territory as an isolated event, the product of a policy of territorial affirmation that followed our continent's independence and tried to put order in the vast and chaotic land recently confronted with the responsibility of organizing sovereign nations. None of this takes away the fact that it was a plundering. One might argue in the same way that the purchase of Alaska several years later from Russia was the beginning of a conquest of what lay north of the Bering Strait—an absurd claim.

Under those circumstances territorial confrontations were frequent, not only in the north of the continent but everywhere; and Peru was no exception. After the conflicts with Mexico and the U.S. Civil War, the United States turned inward until the final decade of the century. England, then, was the major foreign presence in the Latin American independent republics. Although after the definitive break with Spain, the base of this presence was economy rather than politics, especially as regards capital. We have seen how the British participation developed in Peru's economy.

U.S. isolation ended in 1889. That was when the United States launched its "good neighbor" policy aimed at creating military and political alliances in the Western Hemisphere. From that time, when the United States was already a world economic power and its capital had been involved in Latin American economy for years (in Peru, for example, it financed the railway), interventionist inclinations were evident. They were almost the natural extension of North American capitalist dynamism. The key year in the history of relations between Latin America and the United States is not 1823 or 1846, but 1898. This is when the United States became a decisive factor of political power in the Americas with its "splendid little war," which expelled the Spaniards from Cuba and Puerto Rico and created de facto a direct zone of influence for Washington in Latin American affairs. From that time on, the Caribbean and Central America were an almost automatic point of reference concerning Washington's foreign policy. Although the rest of the continent also saw gradual U.S. intervention in its political life, it was never as great as in the Caribbean and Central America. That was the year that the Atlantic replaced the Mediterranean as the axis of universal politics. Latin America, nailed in the heart of this new radius of political influence, became a part of the "U.S. zone." From that moment, Latin America became divided between that fascination-emulation that Uruguayan José Enrique Rodó called *nordomanía*[3] and a hate for the bully north (and an envy of the successful north). The United Fruit banana plantations, the Panama Canal, and the repeated military interventions between 1904 and 1933 in the Dominican Republic, Cuba, Honduras, Nicaragua, and Haiti became symbols of new relationships between the United States and its neighbors.

From that time on, U.S. policy concerning Latin America has oscillated between two poles. There has been hegemony: the Platt Ammendment, the Roosevelt corollary to the Monroe doctrine, and the Johnson Doctrine of 1966. And there has been condescension: Roosevelt's "good neighbor" policy in 1933, Kennedy's Alliance for Progress in the 1960s, and the Carter "human rights" thrust in the 1970s. The last one punished human rights violators on the right, but was extremely lenient with those on the left. And so U.S. foreign policy became part of U.S. domestic policy. There were those convinced of the need to face by any means necessary "anti-U.S." values south of the Rio Grande. They were the nation's patriots. And there were the "nice guys" who carried out foreign policy with a guilt complex over imperialist evils of the past or for having obtained an economic success that the south of the continent lacked. Peru, like its neighbors, was affected by both policies. However, it did not suffer the consequences of imperialism as such thanks to geographic reasons and what was considered its lesser strategic weight in the region.

Peruvian political and university culture was filled with anti-U.S. feelings in the last decades, just like on the rest of the continent. The 1980s brought in new policies, which anti-U.S. propaganda deformed out of a visceral hate for Ronald Reagan. While instruments used by some specific members of the U.S. administration during that era shocked public opinion in that country (and even broke the law), it is clear that from the point of view of those interested, that is, Latin Americans, we saw a change with respect to the past: there was an active defense of liberal democracy. In contrast to the past when the containing of communism was shored up by military dictatorships or direct military intervention on the part of the United States, this new stage saw Washington trying to defend itself against communism in the region via something more in line with its own values: democracy. So while at the beginning of the first Reagan administration only 30 percent of the continent was in democratic hands, by the time we reached the 1990s the figure was at 90 percent. There were such important results as the anti-*sandinista* victory in Nicaragua and the peace agreements in El Salvador. The case of Panama—related to drug dealing and something the United States considers a piece of its domestic policy and national security—is special. However, that decade left a bad taste in peoples'mouths once again in the history of our relation. It was as though the United States was not working as an equal with its neighbors, but from a position of command and hegemony, although its means were different. Once again as well, the turbulent relations between Americans and Latin Americans became part of a complicated political confrontation with Washington, leaving a large number of bruises and wounds.

This is the context in which we see a transformation of the relationship in the 1990s. The scenario offers the United States a new Latin America that has become almost completely democratic. Communism has turned into a museum piece, as it learns to lay down its arms and get along with the system. There is a new generation of leaders trying—with greater or lesser emphasis, quickly or slowly—to apply market principles so long associated with the criminal exploitation of our wealth by foreigners— first, the Spaniards, then the English, then the Yankees. In addition, it has become clear that a military dictatorship is no way to struggle against drug dealing, because the corrupting force of such a business offers great benefits for this type of system.

Coinciding with this new political map there is a growth in commercial tension among the large economic blocks (Asia, Europe, the United States). Suddenly, the United States begins to see Latin America as an exciting possibility: an economic opportunity compensating for difficulties in gaining access to the European and Japanese markets and the self-centered nature of the inward looking entities occupying the European and Japanese space. This new focus has begun to dissipate the atavism of a rhetoric that had traditionally blamed Latin American poverty on the wealth of the United States. Such a sophism was for a long time a bone of contention between the two parties and is still a source of mistrust. Figures demonstrate that this was not remotely true. In 1950 U.S. investments in Latin America amounted to $4 billion, a trifle. In 1965 the amount was $11 billion, still a modest sum. In time, the United States came to invest infinitely more in Canada, Europe, and Japan. In recent years scarcely 5 percent of U.S. investments have gone abroad and only some 7 percent of its production has been exported. Seventy percent of its foreign investment has gone to developed countries, while the remainder was divided among countries referred to as Third World. Latin America managed to gather the crumbs of this activity. The great transnationals (General Electric, General Motors, etc.) sell ten times more per year within the United States than in the Third World. In addition, the notorious trade deficit of the United States means that the country exports less than it imports. So it slowly becomes clear among the Latin American republics that our problem is not U.S. economic imperialism, but, rather, the absence of large quantities of U.S. capital and products within our borders. This coincides with a political mentality that is beginning to see foreign capital as a source of national wealth and imports as a stimulus to competition and a benefit for the lord and master of the market: the consumer, that is, each and every citizen.

Within this novel framework of relations we find President Bush's Initiative of the Americas launched in 1990. It was aimed at creating a free-trade zone throughout the region. The rhetorical reception was positive; but it has still not managed to bring about a continental accord regarding such a zone. Specific countries like Chile have begun to negotiate, as Mexico did earlier on, an economic relationship along the above lines. We are beginning to discover that there are national interests that can be served by an understanding with the United States. For example, a number of Latin American countries realize that if the free-trade zone is not extended and remains confined to the north, several of the preference accords that give them access to the U.S. market (the General System of Preferences, the Caribbean Basin Initiative, the Andean Trade Preference Initiative, which also affects Peru, etc.) will be reverted. And there are cases like Brazil, which, according to the World Bank, will suffer the bulk of trade reduction between the United States and South America if the free zone in question is not broadened.

In light of these realities the wounds of the past are slowly healing. We are beginning to lose our fear of friendly relationships with the neighbor to the north. The bad blood between us is becoming a thing of the past. But it is a fine and delicate task where old resentments are still smoldering. Any incident, no matter how minor, can spark the old anti-imperialist sentiments.

It is within this context that we should see the response of the United States regarding the Peruvian regime as of 5 April 1992. We can leave aside the minor details: the presence of the under secretary of state for Latin American affairs during the Bush administration, Bernard Aronson, in Lima on the day of the coup; or the presence at the Government Palace of Charles Brayshaw, the U.S. Embassy Chargé d'Affairs, when Fujimori returned to the Palace on 13 November 1992 after having to take "refuge" because of a coup attempt (which turned out to be, according to all indications, a farce engineered to cover up a settling of accounts within the army and prevent potential countercoups). In both cases officials have talked about "mere coincidence," claiming that the interviews were scheduled previously. There has been insistence in both cases that it was not a question of solidarity with the dictatorial regime. We have no reason to believe otherwise, but the capacity of U.S. diplomats to be taken by surprise in the least likely place at the least likely moment is odd.

For the United States, Peru posed a more complicated problem than Haiti. It was possible that unilateral statements or measures would upset the continent or cause antagonism owing to what could be seen as Washington's overbearing involvement in the situation and competition with the Latin American governments, be it with the Organization of American States (OAS) or the Río Group. However, President Bush had an initial reaction against any violation of constitutional order in Latin America, be it on the right or left. He said on 6 April that he was "a little concerned" over developments in Peru. On that same day the White House was more firm: it called the coup "a regrettable step backward for democracy." On 10 April George Bush said that Peru should be pressured from abroad, in an obvious call to Latin America. He compared the Peruvian and Haitian crises and spoke of suspending economic aid to Peru, showing a stronger will to pressure the hesitant Latin governments to force a return to democracy in Peru. It was constantly evident that George Bush knew that a sharper tone could endanger the new network of relationships being worked out with his neighbors. So he referred to Peru with his eye on Mexico, Buenos Aires, and Caracas, concerned about the effect his words might have outside of Peru. On Sunday, 12

April, before the first OAS meeting in Washington, George Bush came out for economic sanctions. Two days later Secretary of State James Baker addressed the assembly with especially strong words against Peru. He was confident that Venezuela, Costa Rica, and Argentina with which Washington had been in contact in order to coordinate action, would back him up. But as of 12 April there were symptoms that the diplomatic bureaucracy, personified by Bernard Aronson, was thinking of something different. Aronson told CNN television that Peru must not be isolated but brought back into the democratic sphere. This position coincided with the timid stances of the Latin American foreign ministeries and the corporative and bureaucratic attitude of the State Department in general. The United States finally canceled its economic aid, some $320 million, and reduced its military aid to $30 million. It announced as well the indefinite suspension of this type of assistance. In Lima the embassy followed instructions from Washington and moved on the side of the democratic opposition, but within a sense of prudence. As the days went by, Washington's pressure, which obviously did not mobilize the Latin American governments into punitive measures against Peru, slackened, opting for a *modus vivendi*. There was no backing for the dictatorship, but there was a naive credulity toward the "democratic calendar" established by the Peruvian regime. The State Department suffered from a binary vision of the Peruvian crisis. Between Fujimori and *Sendero Luminoso*, it seemed to opt for the former. Between Fujimori and any military man, it preferred a civilian dictator. Between a nonelected dictator and an elected one, it preferred one chosen in fair elections.

Peru was not important enough for Washington to endanger its relations with the rest of the continent. It opted, therefore, for the least of all the evils. Fujimori became, in the hallways of U.S. bureaucracy, the least of all evils, despite the fact that on paper and in certain official gestures there was open disapproval. There was a revival of the old tendency of U.S. foreign policy to understand the Latin American approach as a counterpoint between a lesser evil and a worse evil, and not between the very democratic values that the United States embodies and the odd forms of political barbarism that, as different as they might seem, are expressions of the same evils. The gestures continued to seem guided by principle, as when on 18 June at the Earth Summit in Rio de Janeiro Bernard Aronson explained that Washington was tired of so many setbacks in the calendar for a return to democracy. But contradictory signals coming from the diplomatic field continued. On 28 August 1992 at an OAS meeting studying Fujimori's calling of elections for a Constituent Congress Bernard Aronson refused even to receive people from the democratic opposition (members of the dissolved Parliament) trying to denounce the shortcomings of the electoral process in question.

There were three motives that were blocking more coherence and firmness in Washington's opposition to the Peruvian regime. The clue to the first is in statements made by National Security Advisor Ben Scowcroft who, in the first weeks after the coup, told CNN television that Fujimori presented a problem because he was carrying out by nondemocratic means many things necessary for Latin America, among them a greater economic opening. The response to this reasoning came from James Baker himself, who said that Fujimori had destroyed Peruvian democracy under the pretext of saving it. But the statements of Scowcroft betrayed how delicate this affair was for the United States. Washington had always favored greater reforms based on an opening and an adherence to the market as well as a struggle against subversion and corruption. So how could it oppose the coup d'état without simultaneously discarding the general reforms in Peru? At least on paper, they seemed to be worthy of the approval Washington had given to democratic governments on the continent. This hesitance, which has to do with a broader perspective encompassing the whole Latin American region, restrained the U.S. government. It sprang from a vision that is simplistic, not well informed, and certainly naïve regarding what is behind the Peruvian regime.

The second factor tempering the U.S. stance resulted from contradictions between the White House and the State Department, despite the fact that Baker himself was more in tune with the Bush line than his subordinates. This duality was nothing new in U.S. foreign policy; in fact, it seems to be a constant. To it, of course, has to be added the duality coming from the fact that Congress itself has a say in such foreign policy decisions as financial aid. In any case, State Department officials did not follow through the initial sternness of the White House, and therefore gave the Peruvian regime breathing space.

But the third factor was the decisive one: the giving in of most Latin American governments to the Peruvian dictatorship. Washington is obsessed with not unearthing the ghosts of the past, so it sacrificed something of its democratic leadership in the face of the Peruvian crisis in an attempt to preserve the recent balance achieved in hemispheric relations. In light of this, one cannot help but remember that the United States has not hesitated to approve and apply the Torricelli Bill (the Cuban Democracy Act), which extends the embargo against Cuba, despite opposition from all the Latin American governments.[4]

The influence in Europe of Washington's foreign policy concerning Latin America is wide. But in the Peruvian case there are some paradoxes. Several European countries have proved more constant and coherent in their pressure against the de facto regime than Washington. Spain, for example, was tougher regarding its condemnation of Peru despite the fact that in 1992 the Spanish government had more than sufficient reason not to antagonize a continent especially sensitive to the commemoration of the discovery of the Americas, the beginning of a painful experience of conquest and three centuries of colonization. Spain suspended economic aid ($162 million), pulled out of the Peru Assistance Group (international backing for the re-incorporation of Peru into the international financial community), suspended negotiations on a cooperation treaty, and decreed an embargo on arms for our country. Germany, besides canceling a Fujimori visit and issuing a fierce multiparty statement from the Bundestag, suspended economic assistance worth 180 million marks and asked the rest of the European Community to take similar action. Only France, whose foreign policy regarding Latin America has included tolerance of dictatorships like Cuba and that of the *sandinistas* in Nicaragua, came out against sanctions. We are speaking of Europe, which does not have the same leadership responsibilities as the United States in the Western Hemisphere. None of these countries was prepared to accept the calendar of the dictatorship. But thanks to the growing foot-dragging on the part of the United States and the OAS, they decided to stand on the sidelines: they were neither in favor nor against the dates set by Fujimori. Spain was quickly forced to lower the tone of its criticism of the Peruvian dictatorship in light of the gradual falling off of Washington's resistance.[5]

The key to the international attitude vis-à-vis the Peruvian regime has been the combined response of the United States and the rest of Latin America. There is a curious situation here. After so many decades when Latin America denounced U.S. interventionism claiming that it was capable of solving its own problems, the Peruvian case makes it clear how much these republics need effective leadership when it comes to meeting antidemocratic threats causing them to tremble with impotence and to take refuge in mediocre and fleeting diplomatic formulas. The forum chosen to address the Peruvian case, one which is in itself a reflection of the relationship between the two poles of the continent, was the OAS.

Today this organization is suffering an identity crisis similar to that of other bodies emerging in the postwar period and unable to find their place within the new order. The difference between the OAS and NATO, for example, is that the latter is faced today with a scenario very different from that in which it operated successfully for four decades. But the American entity has never really had specific weight. Its identity crisis is not owing, then, to the fact that it must now adapt its mechanisms to new realities, but to the fact that realities have changed around it without its having the slightest thing to do with the changes. That is, there is not a proliferation of democracies in Latin America today because the OAS has promoted it. There has not been a change in the nature of relationships between the United States and its neighbors because the OAS has acted as a vehicle of understanding. Nor is economic liberalism in fashion because the OAS has been its standard-bearer. Nor is there civil peace in countries where up until recently families were ripped apart by civil war because the OAS has helped negotiate it.

The OAS is nothing more than a debating club. Its only positive feature lies in its origins, or better said, the good intentions of its precursors and founders. We find its remote antecedents in an 1890 conference in Washington where participants attempted without success to promote a commercial union. How much time it has taken for this idea to catch on again! Similar efforts failed up until 1948 due to the fact that the foreign policies of the nations in question were decided upon outside hemispheric meetings.

Finally in 1948—a Latin American reflection of the postwar era in the wake of the defeat of Nazism and fascism by Western democracies—the OAS was born with the Bogota Charter. It came out for a collective defense of Latin American territory and the promotion of the values of democratic tolerance among nations. But since that time we have seen a proliferation of dictatorships rendering it impossible to make the OAS more than, as I said, a debating society. Only one serious decision was ever taken. It came in 1962 with the exclusion of Cuba. Several years later, in the 1970s, the OAS lifted the ban on Cuba. The country did not rejoin the organization, but the move permitted the different countries to renew diplomatic relations with the Castro dictatorship, something that several of them went out of their way to do.

The OAS was, then, a chimera. Latin America was plagued with nationalist dictatorships that refused to accept regional involvement in their private domain. It also suffered from dictatorships with an internationalist bent; the jungle was a more desirable theater for the promotion of their values than international forums, and guerrilla cartridge belts were better agents of continental defense than the neckties of diplomats. What is more, the OAS itself came to reflect the antidemocratic policies of the nations in question. The dictatorships held forth for a long period of time, so it was impossible to give this mechanism another raison d'étre than that of a sounding board for the very domestic misery of our nations. It need not be stressed that the "realpolitik" of the United States, according to which the containment of communism included alliances with military dictatorships, became one more form of carrying out foreign policy behind the back of the OAS.

The economic philosophy in Latin America during the postwar period became an essential stumbling block for the functioning of a continental mechanism to safeguard libertarian values. A good number of things happened during those years. Argentina saw the ruin of its agricultural production with Perón who was trying to industrialize in order to substitute imports. Social spending quickly broke the bank and the lack of income from agricultural exports made it impossible for the state to have hard currency to import materials that might make possible the creation of certain industries. The structuralist philosophy, strongly influenced by Keynes, contaminated the whole continent. The Argentinian disaster was repeated in a host of countries. This economic nationalism was, along with the dictatorships, a death warrant for the principles of the OAS.

But the democracies coming to the fore decisively on the continent in the 1980s still did not transform the OAS into a continental expression of a common foreign policy backed by the very democratic principles in effect at home. Rather, the OAS was a refuge for the cowardice of each of Latin America's democratic nations. They did not dare to use this hemispheric tool on their own ground to help correct endless political perversions. This explains, for instance, the birth of the Contadora Group, which during these years was charged with dealing with the civil wars in Central America, a place where the OAS did not get involved. That effort was in vain. In the first place, Contadora suffered on a lesser scale from the same lack of coherence regarding principles and political will as the OAS. From Contadora there later emerged the *Grupo de Apoyo*, a larger forum of Latin American countries bent on assisting the Contadora Group, but it was still unable to defend democracy in Central America. It became rather an instrument of anti-U.S. forces in the region. Then the Esquipulas accords in 1987 changed things somewhat when they made democracy the touchstone for pacification in Central America and broadened anti-imperialist demands to include the end of Soviet and Cuban interventionism.

In very recent times, the Latin American democracies have had three serious tests: Cuba, Haiti, and Peru. In all three cases they have been incoherent, weak, and inept. Regarding Haiti, they applied an embargo they refused to apply concerning Peru. When it comes to Cuba, the embargo is defended only by the United States. The Latin American countries (among them such anti-Castro governments as Argentina) refuse to accept it. Several countries have even talked about allowing Cuba to return to the OAS. There has been a consistent weakness concerning Peru that has forced the United States, fearful of souring relations with its new allies, to moderate its position. The first session of the OAS on 14 April refused to demand economic sanctions. Despite the fact that Argentina granted exile at its embassy in Lima to Peru's second vice president, Carlos García y García, who came out against the Fujimori coup, and that Brazil temporarily withdrew its ambassador, these countries did not push economic sanctions in the OAS. There was merely a communiqué calling for a return to democracy and the naming of Uruguayan foreign minister Gros Espiell as special OAS envoy to try to work out a dialogue between the two parties. The two-facedness becomes considerable when we think that in those days there was a decree (13 April) cutting off Peru from the Rio Group (originally the *Grupo de Apoyo* assisting the Contadora effort) in Santiago de Chile. In some cases a respect for "national sovereignty" was invoked. In others it was not. It all depended. This principle was invoked in the Peruvian case, but not in the Haitian case. Argentina felt that getting involved in the internal affairs of Peru violated Lima's sovereign rights, but it was a firm ally of Washington in its struggle against Iraq (in 1992), which, once the troops that invaded Kuwait were defeated, included an exclusion zone and the fomenting of subversive activities against Saddam Hussein. The principle of nonintervention in the affairs of other countries is a pretext and not a conviction in Latin America. They would do well to recall something Albert Einstein said in 1948 when the new postwar order was emerging: "National sovereignty is a luxury which humanity can no longer allow itself."

Gros Espiell defended time and time again the policy of not applying sanctions against Peru; and he stated with a suspicious naïveté in a visit to Lima in May 1992 that according to official surveys the Peruvian government had a popular backing of 72 percent. He called this an "important element which was generally unknown," hinting at compliance with the regime on the grounds of its apparent stability. It was the acceptance on the part of the OAS of a *fait accompli*. This happened around the same time that the Peruvian government refused to receive the OAS Human Rights Commission specifically dispatched to Lima. On 18 May at an OAS meeting in Nassau Fujimori convinced the delegates to back his calendar for a "return to democracy." It was his nth proposal since April, contradicting earlier ones and perfectly improvised to save the day. In the final OAS meeting on the crisis in Peru (August 1992) the group decided to send a team of observers to check up on local elections, which offered the Peruvian government much needed backing to carry on its long-term objectives. The Peruvian democratic opposition was not allowed to participate in this meeting.

Latin American governments were content with minor gestures to ease their guilt feelings. Apart from the above-mentioned cases of Argentina and Brazil, Colombia gave former president Alan García diplomatic exile on his claim that he was being persecuted by Fujimori. Bolivian president, Paz Zamora, said in Beijing that "the cure in Peru was worse than the illness." At the Earth Summit in Rio de Janeiro Fujimori was placed among the dictators, at a distance from the Latin American presidents. But none of these countries proposed any measures against Peru within the OAS, the forum they themselves had chosen to deal with the Peruvian situation. They all ended up rather compliant with the regime through the hemispheric entity. This instrument turned out to be a good alibi. When the governments in question were asked about policy by critics at home they simply answered that they were following the OAS line, as though they themselves were not the authors of that line. The OAS became an abstract entity, unrelated to its members, the perfect refuge for all the Latin American diplomatic misery where no one was personally to blame.

At the July 1992 Summit of Ibero American countries in Madrid the final document had not a single word condemning Peru. Mexico, in keeping with its policy of siding with dictatorships so that the democracies would not interfere with its own antidemocratic realities, had vetoed the statement of condemnation proposed in the closed-door meeting where the points of the document were decided. Regarding the conduct of Uruguayan foreign minister Gros Espiell, the sharpest criticism came from his country's former president, Julio María Sanguinetti. He said the man's main problem was his burning desire to become general secretary of the organization, a post currently held by Baena Soares from Brazil. It says a lot (everything) about the OAS when we see that a diplomat out to lead it feels his ambitions are incompatible with an active policy against a Latin American dictatorship. Lack of action and neutrality are the best routes toward the top diplomatic post in the hemisphere. In practice the alibi spelled complicity.

Only two Latin American countries acted in a decent manner. Venezuela cut off diplomatic relations with Peru, and its president became a strong critic of the dictatorship. And Panama also broke relations with Peru. Costa Rica threatened to follow suit several times, but never did so. The remainder caved in, not surprisingly. The Inter-American Development Bank, for its part, not bothered with political minutiae, decided in mid-1992 to release $21 million in credits that it had held back since the day of the coup. This was the first part of a $200 million dollar loan agreed upon earlier.

The initial toughness of the United States and Europe could have brought down the dictatorship if the Latin American governments had taken brave and coherent decisions based on principles to smother the coup makers. In the absence of such a policy and having used OAS mechanisms to whitewash the regime and make it more acceptable, and in addition render the weak-kneed response of the OAS more decent, Latin America allowed the consolidation of a de facto government and the waning of the provisional character it had had since April 1992.

This conduct ended the cycle that had begun in 1948 with the OAS Charter. Beginning in 1992 the Organization of American States is, for all practical purposes, dead. It will never again be an important factor in a Latin American political crisis. It expresses, now that we are speaking of a new world order able to offer universal guarantees (in this case regional ones) of democracy, the dichotomy between illusion and reality and, even more sadly, between the rhetoric of a guilty conscience and a policy based on fear.

So long as the United States and Latin America cannot find, and do not look for, a new tool for the regional defense of democratic values, the new order will be a dream. Latin America must do away with its complexes brooding in the depths of the collective subconscious, which paralyze it every time we must meet a regional threat from events in any one of our countries. These complexes are probably related to our relations with the United States. It is a sensitivity derived from the historical memory that blocks Latin America from joining with the northern neighbor in common policies that might affect a specific Latin American country emerging as a threat to the new order, that is, as a threat to the others. But there is also the question of certain governments' lack of confidence in their own stability. The Peruvian case is a small laboratory regarding forces that are more or less at play on the rest of the continent. A foreign policy concept, which is more magic than real claims that side-stepping the Peruvian reality and avoiding a confrontation with those forces that are carrying the day will keep them from coming to the surface elsewhere. This is the reasoning in some countries bordering on Peru. They feel that, faced with the possibility of *Sendero* spilling over into their territories, it is preferable to support a dictatorship that can contain it. They also feel that confronting the Peruvian military might mean problems with their own armed forces sparking upheavals at home. Obviously, all this indicates a serious lack of confidence on the part of the new Latin American democracies in their own institutions and a lack of ideological principles and political will to shore up the recent democratic order. Democracy is a reality that they accept and prefer, but they do not have the moral consistency sufficient to develop a permanent and active policy of defense beyond their own borders.

Such psychological weaknesses in the Latin American democracies are a major obstacle concerning the creation of an active consciousness in the region that needs to bring into play a mechanism that might solidify the new order on the short or long term. We spent a long time with the anti-U.S. jeremiad precisely because we wanted to become the masters of our own foreign policy. But now that this is within our grasp, we display a complete inability to meet the challenge. We are still living the childhood of democracy, and are certainly far off from reaching maturity. This is the upsetting truth that Peru has brought out in Latin America. We heard a lot of talk about the 1980s as the "lost decade" because of the economic disaster of our democracies; but the decade was praised a great deal because of that very democratization. Today we verify that also from a foreign policy point of view the 1980s was a lost decade and that the 1990s are beginning poorly.

Owing to one of those coincidences in the history of nations, Peru has brought to light a new factor in the region's foreign policy: Japan. Japanese interest in Latin America is not recent. But the peculiar coincidence that the son of Japanese immigrants is at the center of certain political events has sparked more interest in Japan toward Peru and the continent in general, where for several years there has been silent though systematic Japanese penetration. The Pacific basin, in as much as it is a geographical reality, is also an ongoing communications bridge between the Western coast of Latin America and the East. It is taking on growing political and economic dimensions. This relationship has its extremely ancient roots in the Mongolian hordes, which managed to cross the Bering Strait tens of thousands of years ago. Today the crossing between the two shores of the Pacific comes in the form of *Sogo Shosha* Japanese executives. Japanese capitalism began sniffing about in Latin America some three decades ago. But now, after an interruption caused by the foreign debt crisis of 1982, there is a renewed and high-pressure interest. No one speaks much about this openly in Japan. Since the impositions of MacArthur Japanese foreign policy has been quiet, furtive, and almost with an air of shame. The Japanese have no desire to beat the drums over this historical phase in their relations with Latin America. They don't want to advertise it as the "free trade zone of the Pacific" or anything of the sort. A feature of Japanese foreign policy in this century has been to offer the appearance of casualness and spontaneity regarding decisions that emerge in fact from the computer and have to do with a *raison d'état*.

Latin America is not a priority for Japan. In the minds of the world, it continues to be Washington's backyard. But for the first time the Japanese intuitively figure that this might not always be the case. There are two reasons for it. The economic recession in the north of the hemisphere strengthened Japan's ability to pressure the south, and made the market, where half of Latin America's products go, less attractive, thus encouraging the look for other openings. And in the south there is the adolescence of democracy, which is rapidly turning our old political misanthropy into curiosity, replacing Latin America's aloof tendency to remain economically isolated from other countries with a voracious appetite for the universal map.

In the nineteenth century the Anglo-Saxon world replaced the Latin world south of the Rio Grande as a system of international reference. Today we see the appearance of a third system: the Asian. Japan's penetration has begun diligently, and could become a key factor, so much so that, if a trade zone bridging Alaska and the Tierra del Fuego comes into being in the near future, it might no longer be possible to push the Asian empire aside. In 1991 we saw the first symptoms of growth in Latin America after a pullback in the 1980s, and Japan increased its exports there by 25 percent. This came with a flood of industrial products, from automobiles to machinery and equipment. The current also began to flow in the other direction. Twenty-one percent of Peruvian exports and 12 percent of those from Chile went to Japan. According to The America's Society,[6] nearly 15 percent of Japan's total investment in the world was in Latin America in 1991, amounting to $400 billion. The facts show that there is little chance for the continental free trade zone to stem the Japanese tide, which would probably be the interest of the United States, for there are powerful economic ties being created between the Latin American countries and Japan.

But there is more than capital in the game. Tokyo is not indifferent to the fact that 1 million Japanese live in Brazil and that Peru hosts the second largest Japanese colony in Latin America. Nor is it ignorant of the way in which Japan burst onto the electoral scene in Peru in 1990 as a mythological force carrying votes and hopes. The case of Peru, a Latin American country governed by a son of Japanese immigrants, became an important point in Japanese foreign policy. In the beginning Tokyo was cautious because it knew very little about this man, and because of his rhetorical populism in the second round of elections, which was a bad omen for the future government. Later the Japanese discovered that, after all, Peru could be a beachhead for their penetration of a promising region such as Latin America. The Japanese began to identify with the Peruvian project through credits, political backing, and certain investments. Without a doubt, behind this policy of collaboration there was the hope that their own model might be capable of creating a Latin American (and Third World) miracle. There was also the fear that the Fujimori model might fail and that Japan's competitors would use that failure as a tool to demythify Japanese success.

The coup d'état became a double-edged sword. Japan could force Fujimori to return to democracy and become a decisive factor in the new world order in the region. If this did not come about, Tokyo could be accused of backing an antidemocratic project linked to Japanese interests. Japan's response was cautious. It began by threatening to suspend economic aid to Peru; but then it hid behind the curtains of private diplomacy, sending out periodic signs that it was using discreet pressure on Fujimori. Tokyo even said it was responsible for the fact that Fujimori had offered elections for a constituent assembly. Japan had decided not to sacrifice Fujimori. Since the Peruvian government was completely abandoned internationally, Tokyo's ability to pressure Lima was increased considerably. This ability to pressure Peru served the Japanese interests in the whole region, as long as the pressure did not topple Fujimori. Democracy was a minor detail in this interplay of political and economic interests. Such a scale of priorities is not unusual in Japanese foreign policy regarding Latin America. During the 1970s the Japanese were among the greatest providers of easy money for Latin American military dictatorships. It is true by contrast that during the 1980s Japan helped seek mechanisms to reduce our foreign debt. It is understandable that Japan wanted to take advantage of the occasion to strengthen its Latin American policy given the fact that one of those countries' presidents is from the Land of the Rising Sun. It is also understandable that Japan has found in Peru the perfect scenario to compete with the United States for political influence in the latter's "zone of influence." The sad part is that the price paid was Peruvian democracy. Analyzing its priorities, Japan had to finally decide between democracy and Fujimori. The latter seemed to serve its immediate interests better.

But the Latin American countries bear the final responsibility. What moral authority do we have to demand that Japan abandon Fujimori when the Latin American democracies themselves were not immediately ready for a serious mobilization in favor of Peruvian democracy and the United States, sensitive to the lack of political will on the part of its new allies, preferred to cut off its initial efforts in favor of the cause of freedom in Peru? It is strange that Peru—a country isolated and with a growing lack of importance in the international community owing to the weakness of its institutions and its economy—became the focus of international attention for several months, a center of political curiosity. The reason, of course, was more psychological than anything; Peru was a microcosm of political phenomena taking place around the world and the place were those political forces at work produced the fastest and oddest results, touching a sensitive nerve particularly in the Latin American region. Peru put its neighbors in the hemisphere to the test when it became an international *issue*. And in response to that challenge, the region betrayed a tremendous gap between words and acts in this new democratic era. What was revealed was the weakness of the new order that they were casting to the winds, an unwillingness to take action. This is, in practice, the old order. The countries stood up and took notice of Peru briefly, attracted by strange noises coming from there. Then the covered their ears and did an about-face.

Notes

1. Again, the word *liberal* is taken in the classic sense associated with the defense of freedom in all its forms, not the American sense.
2. Francis Fukuyama, *The End of History and the Last Man* (New York: Free Press, 1992).
3. José Enrique Rodó, *Ariel* (Madrid: Espasa Calpe, 1948). (The first edition appeared in Montevideo, Uruguay, in 1900.)
4. President Clinton's policy toward Peru has not differed much from that of his predecessor. On two occasions, however, the U.S. government has acted firmly, giving some of us hope that it has not completely abandoned the fight for the recovery of democracy in Peru. The first such occasion was during the presentation of credentials by the Peruvian ambassador at the White House, when President Clinton was very critical of the Peruvian de facto regime. The second was in April 1993, when the Peruvian army sent tanks to the streets as a sign of defiance against a very small group of members of the opposition who were trying to investigate human rights abuses, a move that was accompanied by a communiqué in which it was made clear that the army was contemplating the closure of the "Congress of the Geishas". The American embassy protested strongly against the whole affair and let it be known that new sanctions might be ordered if tanks did not go back to the barracks immediately.
5. It is estimated that Fujimori's coup cost Peru $700 million in all, which is the amount Peru would have received during 1992 had there not been any economic sanctions.
6. Susan Kaufman Purcell and Blake Friscia, "A Growing Yen for Latin America," *Hemisfile* (New York) 3, no. 3 (May 1992).

5

The Liberal Option

The Peruvian case brings together several conditions that, by comparison or contrast, shed light upon this new continent, which Latin America appears to want to become. The first of these is the discrediting of democracy. Today we are living what we might call the anticlimax of the democratic euphoria of the 1980s. In a very short ten-year period the democratic system has become associated with the failure of governments, policies, and men that were responsible for the affairs of the state. Or, better said, the Latin American crisis has erased the chronological and psychological border that up until recently separated this new democratic era from the dark dictatorial stage of previous years, as if a reality underlying these changes in the political regime meant the continuation of the same old civil frustrations. The division made by the politicians, journalists, and historians between the democratic decade of the 1980s (and now the 1990s) and the preceding dictatorships does little to impress people who do not feel it on the streets. There are different cases where there were very brutal dictatorships and where an atmosphere of political liberty and freedom of expression mark a contrast that many citizens can feel. But in general, differences in the political climate are not what the average citizen is perceiving, but those in the social and economic reality.

There is a second condition closely tied to this discrediting of democracy. It is the upsetting institutional effect of the popular rejection of the political class and the almost violent emergence of forces, which, sincerely or falsely, present themselves as a balm of newness, freshness, and cure for Peru's rotten political world. This is what is going on in several Latin American countries, and, with different nuances and intensity, even in the United States. In Peru we find the maximum expression of this reality, while elsewhere it takes on less explosive and less revolutionary forms.

The third condition that Peru has as a microcosm of the new Latin American situation is the idea that the country is taking a "liberal" tack, in the classical European meaning of liberalism, that is, a social and economic organization based on the principle of freedom and a free working of market dynamics. The enemies of the Peruvian government accuse it of carrying out a "liberal" or "neoliberal" policy, which has failed previously in Peru and the rest of Latin America, and which places our country at the service of international banking and its political servants, the Western governments. But they add another element: the supposed relationship of mutual dependency between liberalism and dictatorship. And here the Peruvian case once again has Latin American repercussions. Critics of the liberal option point to the Peruvian dictatorship as a natural consequence of the liberalism in fashion today on the continent. And they predict that liberal reform policies elsewhere in the region will turn out to be authoritarian. Those who favor the Peruvian model share a similar criteria from opposite positions. They say the Peruvian case does indicate a serious reform. They do not call it exactly liberal, but they say it is modern in contrast with the populism, socialism, and state control that existed before. On describing their model in a way so reminiscent of the liberal thrust making its way among Latin Americans, they help perpetuate the notion that this reform is truly liberal.

In this way the foundations are being laid for one more misunderstanding in our history, the discrediting of an option not really put into play by confusing it with a reality that has little to do with the principles and reforms that it embodies. The strange truth is that both those in favor of and those against the model are helping to put a liberal label on something that is not liberal, something that has happened previously in our republican life. And so the semantic confusion becomes an ideological confusion. And the ideological confusion ends by bringing about counterproductive political results. At a point where the great Latin American debate centers on the need to adopt liberal policies to reform the heritage of a past where liberalism was absent, this confusion is extremely dangerous.

In Peru, then, we have these three characteristics that, without underplaying their peculiarities (and there are many), form a part of the forces, currents, and phenomena that are flooding the continent, although to different degrees. There is the discrediting of democracy, the emergence of a model as far from the democratic system as it is from the interplay of political parties, and an ideological confusion concerning what this new model really represents in terms of political philosophy and daily practice. It is, in fact, a case of two large issues. One has to do with the instruments at the disposal of society to achieve success. The other has nothing to do with methods or tools, but with objectives. What kind of society do we want for ourselves? The first issue calls into question the ability of democratic institutions, including the powers of the state and the political parties, to lead the nation, no matter in what direction. The second has to do with the goals set by those shaping the new model and with the perception of those goals on the part of leaders pushing toward them as well as of those who question them.

In both cases it is a search, although in both camps there are those who believe they have found what they are looking for. Just like always, the greater portion have been taken in, in their anguished search, by a minority making them believe they have found the promised land. In the first case I leave to one side the coterie involved with the top levels of dictatorial power, seeking what their like has always sought: a monopoly on power. I am interested rather in the attitude of citizens apart from the intimate circle of the presidency who are seeking a system better than democracy. And in the second case, I am interested in those seeking a social model different from that which has always governed their lives. This is not a calm search. It is desperate, conditioned by the urgency of the crisis and the distress of human suffering. But this state of mind has a good side. It could unleash a powerful energy, which, put to good use, could offer Peru the dynamism it needs to drag itself out of the swamp. The way things stand today, however, it is badly channeled. This energy is in the service of policies that many Peruvians have identified as needing change, but which are turning out not to be able to transform reality or to mean anything really new. There is nothing in the model going to the root of the evils of our institutions.

There is the appearance of newness, but certain vices at the heart of the Peruvian problem are perpetuated. The result, then, is total confusion, an overwhelming confusion to which the ruling classes have contributed in two ways: a lack of understanding concerning what is wrong with Peru, and a lack of understanding regarding how to create a different society.

By placing their rhetoric, sophisms, and ideological casuistry at the service of the model in question, they only perpetuate two mistaken ideas that have to do with the two important matters in contemporary Peruvian politics to which I referred above: that the failure of democratic governments means the failure of the democratic system; and that the policies of economic adjustment and liberalization amount to that serious transformation of Peruvian institutions of which the defenders of freedom are in favor. Given the Latin American repercussions of these two matters, we should take a closer look.

New politicians have emerged in Lima, Prague, Manila, Dallas, and elsewhere. They have suddenly and almost at once come to the forefront of politics in their countries. They all owe their existence to a universal feeling of civic impatience; but they differ greatly—they are figures which could have appeared only in their own countries. And they are all tied to that obscure zone where reasons for the success or the failure of their respective nations are to be found. There is very little connection between the tricky little man from Lima's picaresque, the austere Confucian judge in Manila, the Polish exile who almost beat out Lech Walesa, or the U.S. businessman who received 20 million votes in 1992 in the most powerful country on earth. The first and the last on the list are expressions of the societies in question: in one case, of the tenacious historical disaster; in the other, of brillant success. In the U.S. situation it is not surprising to see that the average citizen would imagine a powerful businessman capable of bringing in successful policies in public administration. The joke going around then was, "We're tired of millionaires in the White House. We want billionaires now."

But there is a common factor in these societies opting, boldly or timidly, for politicians with a new face. It is the syndrome of the independent. In the rich countries as well as the poor, in nations where liberty has ruled as well as those where it is a recent conquest, people are asking for something new, not so much regarding policy, but in the way of carrying it out. They seem not to be interested in the content, as much as in a new packaging. Miriam Defensor Santiago in Manila offered no new ways of creating wealth; she offered an ethic for public administration. On the other side of the Pacific Ross Perot (U.S. presidential candidate in 1992) concealed his government program for a number of months, as he found that such conduct was a formidable source of public support. Every time he had the chance, he insisted that the moment had come to bring the traditional politicians down. None of these figures are solid. Their popularity is based on sensation rather than certainty, on intuition rather than conviction, on a rejection of the establishment rather than a calendar of reforms to deal with the actual problems that make voters desperate.

Of course this is not the first time in the course of democratic civilization that societies express weariness in their relationships with power. Throughout a good part of the nineteenth century Western democracy was something reserved for the privileged minorities that could carry it out behind the backs of the others. It was only in 1848 that France established universal suffrage. In England this came about only in 1918. In the United States the full participation of blacks in democratic life emerged only a few decades ago. These periods prior to democratization were plagued by expressions of discontent. They came via socialism and even via militarism. In the first half of the century, in Italy and Germany, the failure of the politicians was a banner for the multitudes following Mussolini and Hitler. In France the mess of the Third and Fourth Republics brought us De Gaulle with his mixture of grandeur and authoritarianism. Later he would be insulted in the streets by mobs chanting Maoist slogans in rejection of capitalist democracy.

There are differences in this new popular backlash against political life. For the moment it is being channeled via the democratic route, with the exception of Third World cases like Peru, and appears to be continuing that way. The process points to a modernization of the system, not to its extinction. They want to clean up politics and finish off the vice of mercantilism, which uses political power to favor the specific fortunes of the most influential. They want to punish corruption and take away the set position it has aquired in public posts. There is no ideology behind this weariness with democracy. No one wants an end to the system, but a renovation. There are social frustrations behind this state of mind, but what is backing it up is not really a social calamity. In the West the last forty years have seen (with exceptions) an unprecedented economic expansion accompanied by a growth of the middle classes. In the United States the 1980s brought about a period of abundance. The times of political hobbyists and political skepticism that we are experiencing today do not imply, as they did in the past, that the masses are about to engage in revolution and follow sinister tyrants (at least in the developed world).

This does not mean that the phenomenon is less intense. Let us not forget that the French Revolution was the result of a frustration much more political than economic. Perot is not a child of U.S. poverty. He comes rather from a society that for a long time was involved in its own affairs and in creating wealth without too much concern about who governed or how they governed except when the IRS came around to collect taxes. Societies are moving toward a political culture that wants to bring back the Athenian flavor it had in its remote origins when democracy was not exercised vicariously, but directly in the public square. Even in the underdeveloped world where there are strong economic factors to be considered, there is today this spirit of participation behind the phenomenon of political hobbyists.

But our societies will discover many things. It is not possible, for example, to reproduce the city of Athens in the gigantic nations of our times. Political power, as Machiavelli laid out very clearly, is not the kingdom of God. It is an enclave of particular codes, which are almost impossible to break or change. Business and state affairs are two different things in form and substance. The one must be the free interplay of private interests, if it is to be authentic; the other, the realm of general principles. This does not mean, of course, that there should be no involvement of interests in government and of principles in business. It is too great a risk for the men today enjoying the favor of antipolitical people to end up as politicians and for us not to demand that they show some sort of public government commitment. If we let this pass, the most clever opportunists and demagogues will take over. Our very democracy as a form of government is in danger. The feeling of rejection of traditional politics could overflow within the system, backed by this exquisite dictatorial form consisting of an alliance of the powers that be with the masses over the heads of politics and politicians.

As we see, there is a relationship between the phenomenon of weariness with the political class in the developed Western world and in Latin America. There are important differences among the Latin American republics. Venezuela and Colombia, for example, were able to establish in recent decades a democratic consensus among their political classes, and have managed stability. After the fall of dictator Pérez Jiménez in 1958 Venezuela saw a give and take between the two traditional parties: Democratic Action and COPEI. The first leaning more to the left, and the second more to the right, to date they have offered that democracy stability. In Colombia in the 1950s there was the historical Sietges (Spain) Pact. Here the liberals and conservatives who had spent a century in civil wars decided to throw out a dictator and to rotate in power in a democratic form for sixteen years. The people ratified the party agreement via elections. In time the parties competed for power in a normal fashion. This democratic culture, stronger than that in Peru, is what has allowed the countries in question to face the current weariness with the political class without going beyond the constitutional framework, although there have been coup attempts like the ones in Caracas. The democratic institutional consensus has prevented the fall of Venezuelan democracy.

But paradoxically the two-party system in both countries is in and of itself a factor in the erosion of the political class. This system is falling apart in Colombia, for example, with the emergence of forces like the former M-19 guerrilla, which has been brought into civil life. By contrast, in Bolivia the pact between the MIR of President Paz Zamora and the movement of former military dictator-turned-democrat Hugo Banzer known as the "Patriotic Agreement," while being a more recent arrangement than those of the other countries, has offered Bolivian democracy stability in these past years. And it appears to be satisfying the electorate; for the moment it is blocking the emergence of any wild card third force able to rise to power, as the 1993 general elections have shown, in which the traditional MNR won, followed by the Patriotic Agreement. The independant candidate came in a distant third.

In Argentina and Mexico with the traditional justicialista and PRI parties respectively, we see something else taking place. The parties themselves are slowly moving toward modernity and casting aside many of the policies that made up their ideological credo for decades. They are keeping one step ahead of the possibility that some new force might take up the banner of modernity. In the Mexican case there are also such antidemocratic factors as the power structure of the official party, a real state within a state.

In Peru, on the other hand, there has not been a democratic stability that could give the system the possibility of defending itself in the face of the noncredibility of the political class. Nor has the most traditional party, the APRA, carried out political renovations along the lines of what Carlos Menem did with Peronism in Argentina. The political culture in Peru has shown itself weak in defending democracy in the face of adversity, indicating a lack of confidence in the instruments of the system, among them the parties and their leaders. We cannot discard the possibility that if Latin American political classes cannot meet squarely the problems of state political patronage, mercantilism, the *caudillo* tradition, and corruption, which have eaten away at their authority in the eyes of the people, forces seeming more modern and remote from the past will be successful in "independent" experiments bringing down the democratic system. Nor can we discard something different: the upsurge of large independent movements with sufficient strength to take power via the democratic route. This is what happened in Peru. In contrast to Fujimori, they might rule within the system, making it better and stronger. To date, this has not happened in any Latin American country, and the forces emerging in opposition to the political class so far share an antidemocratic ethos.

In Latin America, and the case of Peru is paradigmatic, the problem of the political parties is intimately linked to the problem of the state. The important parties have been one of two things: political forces proscribed by military dictatorships and hardened by underground work and civil insurgence (the APRA in Peru); or state parties that never differentiated between government and state, and that on coming to power took over everything, themselves becoming generators of income and of official and semi-official norms to govern civil life.

Our traditional parties have passed through the two stages: illegality and control of the state. This has perpetuated among them a series of practices related to endemic public vices. The divorce between the people and the state in Peru has directly affected relationships between the electorate and the parties. The latter, even if they are not in government, are seen as an excrescence of the world of political power, extensions of the state, organic structures of a bureaucracy having nothing to do with the people.

Something similar is happening with Accion Democrática in Venezuela where in the 1990s the governing party has been hurt by the disrepute of a state that is seen only as a source of wealth for those in power. The crisis of the party, in Peru and other parts of Latin America, is the crisis of the state. The phenomenon of popular subversion against official Peruvian institutions comes, as we have seen, from a lack of communication and resentment between the power structure and civil society. The political parties, instead of becoming the agents of the people's discontent with the national state, became gears in the traditional machinery and therefore a target of the popular rejection of everything perceived as an official institution.

The Peruvian case combines the popular subversion against traditional politics with the idea that, to a greater or lesser extent, the country, together with its Latin American neighbors, is on a liberal track. It has been said that the liberals are governing in Latin America, that hiding in the woods among the civilian governments in this fin de siècle liberals are exercising power in the Americas. No liberal has won a single election anywhere, but those who have won are often seen as vicars of liberalism, of those ideas that appear to be sweeping with the strength of a maelstrom across lands where not long ago they were despised.

Only now that my own country has sunk into political prehistory; that Venezuela has seen the shrinking of the gigantic figure of its president; and that Brazil is slowly losing the democratic impulse that brought Fernando Collor de Mello to power in 1990, as well as the desire to continue being Brazil, is it becoming clear that what is governing today in Latin America is not liberalism, a total and serious reform of social institutions based on liberty. It is, rather, a tricky hybrid where there is a mixture of certain announcements of liberal change, the odd intuition regarding what is wrong, a logic of budget additions and subtractions, and indignant doses of conformity with the establishment and the legacy of the state. It is precisely because this form of governing cannot be called liberalism that the streets of Venezuela boil over with coup attempts, that Alberto Fujimori knocked off democracy with a cold stab in the back, and that the worst is to be feared in Brazil.

The primary reason for the current Latin American failure is in the bogus roots of the majority of their governments. They are the result of an incredible cajolery that made it possible for the very people who censured liberalism when it was necessary to beat it at the polls, and who received the enthusiastic response of the people due to their use of old style populist politics, to introduce a certain air of common sense in the res publica. When it was clear that there were no more resources, internal or external, to keep paying for populist policies, they rushed, with no convictions, understanding, public backing or a team to make things work, to apply a few pocket "liberal reforms." In so doing, they moved into a bastard terrain. Their political legitimacy became a joke. They firmly believed that power was a convenient substitute for legitimacy and an exemption from the sin of deception. We saw the results of this in the referendum of December 1992 in Uruguay called by the president to get a popular backing for the policy of privatization, that is, a backing for a policy for which he had not asked a mandate in his 1989 election campaign. People were not ready to buy an about-face of this nature and 72 percent of the population voted against it. Like President Lacalle, many Latin American presidents are trying free market policies for which they do not have a mandate, something that gives reform the air of deception and political treason. They forget that as important as the reform of the state is the reform of the minds. And for that, a new, open, honest type of politics is needed, whereby presidents communicate the need and significance of free market reforms before they get to power.

And here we find the first disaster. Since they had not come to power mouthing liberalism, once their electoral credos were abandoned, they decided to make an about-face causing a confusion, which attributed liberal characteristics to their governments. Not everything that is not associated with populism is liberal. Those governments that froze public spending and thinned out tariffs took in a little more in taxes and eliminated subsidies, leaving populism far behind; but they did not even scratch the surface of liberal reform, the essence of which is very distant from the glacial mathematic efficiency of budgetary accounts. This order in the management of the res publica is, without a doubt, necessary as a parallel step toward liberal reform; but it moves on a macroeconomic plane, while liberalism has to do essentially with microeconomics.

The Fernando Belaunde government in Peru, early in the 1980s, was much more responsible in financial management than its successor, and it also decreed an important reduction of import tariffs. But that government was neither liberal nor successful. The confusion led by the betrayal of Fujimori is in part responsible for the fact that liberal ideas have been for the moment prostituted and discredited by his actions. In the case of Venezuela we have a country with an annual growth rate of 10 percent in 1991 and almost 6 percent in 1992, a moderate (for Latin America) inflation rate of 30 percent and a petroleum production level of 2.3 million barrels a year. But this does not automatically mean that it is a liberal society. Quite the contrary. The country is richer than its neighbors, making it more necessary to promote liberalism and expand property and business for all. The fact that this is not taking place explains why Venezuelans are fed up with their politicians.

The International Monetary Fund (IMF), to which our governments have gone running, is not a source of liberalism: it is a source of healthy finances. It is crucial for us to understand the difference. The IMF cards have been played several times in Latin America and this has produced nothing but frustration, because the actions were not backed up by a liberal reform allowing for an attack on the roots of that administrative disorder called inflation, debt, and many other things. The IMF allows governments to stay alive, while liberalism nourishes peoples and societies. The mistake stems from the idea that state financial disorder is not tied to those functions that the state usurps and to institutions serving social development, but to pure administrative clumsiness, bureaucratic carelessness, or the foolishness of particular officials. The truth is that this administrative disorder is a symptom of something much deeper and has to do with the draining of energy and resources, which the state perpetuates with its takeover of the space of civil society. And so the permanent solution is not a mere squaring of accounts, but a reformation of social institutions, the target today of so much popular anger. This is a complex reality that is difficult to explain. It does not fall within simple formulas, and least of all can it be taken on by a society with politicians who look down on communication between ideas and the people.

A policy of adjustment is common among today's Latin American governments. A confusion that is both semantic and ideological calls this thrust "liberal." Fujimori's Peruvian government is no exception to the fashion of economic adjustment policies. More than an ideological conversion or a sudden revelation, these policies are the result of an obligation that reality has imposed on today's rulers in Latin America. These rulers have taken power only to find empty coffers, budgets with no money to cover them, crushing economic commitments, and soaring debts, making it impossible for them to comply with the populist promises that brought them to power. Here, besides Fujimori, we find Carlos Menem and Carlos Andrés Pérez. Despite themselves, many of these populist candidates who became the administrators of austerity discovered a truth that liberals are almost tired of preaching: the key economic responsibility governments have in provoking economic crises and the fact that the average citizen has been robbed of great portions of his income through the most brutal tax of all, inflation. When he came to power, Fujimori was faced with an annual inflation rate of almost 8,000 percent. This was not far from what Nicaragua's Violeta Chamorro found when she became president. The devastating effects of inflation in the Peruvian economy and social life made it obligatory for anyone succeeding the Alan García government to stop the chaos immediately as a first priority. Not doing so would make it impossible to rule, because what was really ruling was inflation. The fiscal madness of the Peruvian system forced Fujimori at once to bring in shock therapy policies, even though his battle cry in the electoral campaign had been precisely a condemnation of shock tactics attributed to the Democratic Front program: cuts in public spending, a traumatic devaluation of money, a suppression of subsidies, a reduction of tariffs, and the firing of thousands of public employees. With certain variations, this has been the line followed by a good number of Latin American governments. In the case of Peru, the monthly inflation rate was brought down to a single digit number digit, varying between 4 and 8 percent.

The adjustment policies in Latin America, generally owing to agreements with the International Monetary Fund, are not an option: they are an obligation imposed by the inheritance of the welfare states. But there is a political perversion out to make these policies an ideological option to meet the challenge of socialism. This creates a false split between socialism and economic adjustment policies, whereby the latter are incorrectly called "liberal." The fact is that any sort of government—rightist, leftist, socialist, conservative—would have to apply adjustment policies under current circumstances for reasons I have mentioned. The inheritance making shock policies necessary can be blamed on the left as much as the right. Despite ideological differences among them, our governments have all with time prolonged the evils at the root of the current crisis. In the eyes of the liberal option, the adjustment policy is scarcely a first step. It is indispensable, but fatally insufficient if it is not accompanied by a vast reform of state institutions. Putting a liberal label on economic adjustment can allow the adversaries of liberalism to discredit for a long time something that has not yet been really brought into play. The majority of the governments carrying out these macroeconomic stabilization policies are not doing so within the context of a serious reform of state-society relationships.

Is it posible to carry out such reforms within a democratic system, or must we depend on a Pinochet or Mexico's PRI or the gang of military men that has taken over in Peru? It is possible, provided there is an unequivocal electoral mandate standing on a vision shared between the rulers and the ruled. (What is not so certain is that such proposals can win elections!) And the reforms must be made seriously, because another staple feature in contemporary Latin American politics, apart from the absence of truth, is half-baked and timid reforms. The Peruvian case is exemplary. From its first days, Mr. Fujimori's government announced the privatization of 300 public enterprises—all of them carryovers from the unfortunate times of General Velasco. This reform is still waiting its turn. It evaporates by the day among the clouds of political contingency, government incompetence, executive cowardice, and the conveniences of that divorce-proof marriage that exists between state control and corruption. Although several enterprises, development banks, the electric company, the national airline, and a number of refineries—were announced for sale at the end of 1992, two and a half years after Fujimori's coming to power legitimately and nearly a year after his coup, only one of them, HierroPerú, has been privatized. The vast majority of public enterprises are still weighing the country down.

In addition, there has been no case of using the instrument of privatization to spread private property among Peruvians, while this has been done successfully in parts of Central and Eastern Europe liberated from communism. And it was carried out, of course, in a spectacular form in England under former prime minister Margaret Thatcher. The concentration of property in a few hands is one of the worst things that can happen to a country out to form a strong civil society and offer its democracy content and stability, because the essence of democracy is property. It is the embodiment of freedom and without it the word makes little sense. We have already seen how in Peru legality is a privilege. The concentration of property in only a few hands is the epiphenomenon of such a reality. Public enterprises are potentially a source of distribution of property, if governments disperse the ownership among masses of citizens, offering them a stake in business activity. There are various mechanisms for bringing this about, which need not be mentioned in detail here. Giving the poor of Peru the option to participate in privatized business is one way of bringing a larger number of citizens to the realm of property and business activity. Such is the essence of the market system and a guarantee of democracy. Of course this participation cannot be a gift. It is possible to offer bonds to be paid immediately or on time according to the possibilities of the buyer. With a bit of imagination, privatization in Latin America can indeed entail a social function. Unfortunately, even partial privatization in the Latin American economies is still a mechanism through which governments simply leave off their fattening of the budget deficit. This is a healthy fiscal principle; but it is not a serious effort to turn more citizens into owners.

The Peruvian government's efforts to do away with the waste of public money are weak indeed, as befits any dictatorship whose stability depends on the amount of popular support it appears to muster. In many instances, the money saved with the right hand is squandered with the left hand. For example, the Fujimori government backed a proposal of Agriculture Minister Absalón Vásquez Villanueva whereby the state would pay out $150 million in farm credits, subsidies for firms, and cooperatives in the countryside via the so-called Rural Banks. At the same time, licenses on the import of agricultural products went up. The effect: unfair competition between subsidized enterprises and others forced to cover costs with no one's help, and a distortion of prices with the consumer suffering the consequences. In this area a solid and necessary reform, the authorization for the creation of limited liability stock companies in the Peruvian countryside, was blocked by the old interventionist practices. In the same way, the 1992 budget was reduced to 5.2 billion soles (approximately $4 billion) in accordance with a healthy principle of austerity in managing the res publica. Unfortunately there was still a deficit amounting to one-fifth of the budget, and there were no foreign credits to compensate for the negative balance.

And so, economic adjustment policies headed in the right direction lacked coherence and daring. But the most serious liability was that the policies were not accompanied by an institutional reform to give Peruvians legal access to the sources of the creation of wealth, the only way to recover from the severe recession caused by the adjustments. In light of Peru's economic paralysis, the state has taken refuge in the same old method used by all the country's populist governments when they have needed money: a hike in gasoline and fuel prices, making everything else more dear in turn. In the absence of an economic growth that can increase tax revenue for the state, the Peruvian government has become a prisoner of the old vicious circle: lack of investment, lack of returns, new taxes, and more recession.

Also announced was a deregulation aimed at ending the morass of Peru's economy and simplifying the Cretan labyrinth hindering the productive life of the country. But the bulk of these regulations are still in place. They burden the life of the country in the municipalities, the ministries, the Palace of Justice, and the public registries. There was supposed to be a transfer of the bureaucracy—1.5 million people—to the market economy. But the majority of those people are still there, despite layoffs in such entities as social security, amounting to an insignificant percentage of public employees, while the productive paralysis makes it impossible for these individuals to opt for private activity. It is useless to claim that the individual is privileged as opposed to the state, that there is economic freedom instead of a command economy, that private enterprise can thrive as opposed to collectivism, or that the consumer is preferred to the functionary if there is no willingness (with all the sacrifice and immense promise that this entails) to reform the state in its entirety. What is announced as a liberal policy ends up being a compromise policy, but limping on both legs. This is a threat to authentic liberal reforms in Latin America as great as what populism has offered in our century, because the enemies of liberalism have created in the political imagination of the continent an association between these programs of macroeconomic adjustment and reforms based on freedom. The failure of the first, because they are insufficient, results in a failure of the second.

I recall a meeting we had in 1990 in Brazil with former president Fernando Collor de Mello. He had just been elected over his socialist rival, Lula da Silva. At that meeting Collor spoke, in his characteristic sportive manner (President Bush compared him to Indiana Jones), of a vast Latin American privatization. It is almost with shame that I look back today on that single steel mill that his turbulent government was able to privatize, and which was the exceptional liberal service record of a president out to modernize his nation. And it is with more shame that I look upon the corruption that smeared his government after an election campaign that had blasted the *marajás* of Brazilian politics. And I ask myself: will Venezuela ever dare privatize the state petroleum company which has been the greatest source of corruption in that country since the days of dictator Juan Vicente Gómez, early in the century, and of course, in the 1970s, when petro-dollars allowed it to take on massive proportions?

And I wonder if the self-styled liberal Salinas de Gortari—who took a great step ahead in tearing apart the *ejido*,[1] that dismal attempt at agrarian reform—would be capable of turning over the energy-rich subsoil of his country to market freedom. After denouncing the vices of the Mexican past, among them corruption, the most natural thing would be to privatize the petroleum industry, which, since the times of Lázaro Cárdenas in the 1930s, has been a source of incredible corruption. And we could review one by one all the enterprises that Latin American governments harbor out of "strategic" considerations. This fatal ideological sophism has been the alibi of hundreds of nationalizations by military and civilian governments bent on not seeing that the capacity for a country's defense is directly linked to its material and technological force, and that this is inversely proportional to the antimodern barbarism of state control. Over and above technical, profitability, and efficiency considerations, what causes many of the Latin American governments that privatize businesses not to give up the most important ones is the old conception of economic nationalism.

The Latin American liberals have still not been able to win elections, but they have been able to set the terms for political debate. They have pushed the role of the state to item number one on the agenda. Peru is no exception. The 1990s have seen how this essential theme has come to the top of the list of priorities and how the political class is taking positions in the debate. The polemic is emerging all around the world. The recent falling apart of the communist model has led to the conviction in the West, among liberals, conservatives, and social democrats, that the state cannot be an agent of the nation's prosperity. Many political parties and intellectuals in the developed countries are coming out in favor of a strengthening of civil society in the face of an intervening state. But they believe, on the other hand, that in the underdeveloped world with its scandalous misery the state has a much more decisive role to play in economic growth. In Latin America as well, those wanting to give the state greater responsibilities in the life of the nation—apart from those it already has, and which it carries out so poorly that it has become alien to the lives of so many—believe that the liberal state is a luxury only rich nations can enjoy. They are falling into a dangerous trap. They cannot recognize that prior to them dozens of generations of Latin Americans guided by exactly the same considerations built the states we are suffering from today in an attempt to become the vast providers of employment, health, education, infrastructure, and social security—in two words: wealth and equality. Many of the founders of Latin American welfare states, Peru included, were part of regimes with absolute powers. This allowed them to use not only resources, but also force, leaving little excuse for their failure. Today the state has fallen apart, and a good portion of the life of the nation is lived behind its back. Despite a massive force, it cannot make itself obeyed.

As a result there is a strange combination of authoritarianism and anarchy. The disaster of the welfare state is such that the enemies of the liberal state accuse the traditional Latin American state they themselves helped build of being just that: a liberal state. And it is not difficult for them to avoid responsibilities regarding the state we have inherited, because it is an entity that has not achieved a single one of the just objectives that the socialists and the populists attribute to an ideal state. It is a fascinating phenomenon. The misery of the Peruvian State is such that those responsible do not recognize themselves as part of it. And what is more, the all-pervading deficiency of the Peruvian state means it is unable to provide those things that are its responsibility. And so, many liberals are in the paradoxical position of demanding more state action in many areas.

The essential mistake is believing that the state is an autonomous entity independent from the nation with its own resources to be divided providentially among the citizens being governed. Such is not the case. The state is interlocked with the nation to which it belongs, and its resources are the property of that nation. So for the state to have resources, it must get them from a nation that is prospering. This dependency relationship between state resources and the society from which it collects them should serve to place the creation of wealth at the top of the political agenda. If the arguments of freedom are not sufficient to convince Latin American socialists or conservatives that civil society must breathe freely in the creation of wealth, there is the argument of necessity: the state can survive financially only if citizens generate the prosperity that eludes them today.

A terrible mistake is at the heart of the system that our elders have left us: the belief that the resources of the state are the offspring of providence, in other words, the belief that states never fail. To a certain extent, this is true: states never fail, because they can always obtain money by expropriating it directly or indirectly from the citizen, falling into debt or inventing it. The massive inflation that hit Peru during the Alan García administration, just like Bolivia under Siles Suazo or Nicaragua under Daniel Ortega, has opened the eyes of certain political sectors concerning the harmful relationship between the capacity of the state to generate resources in a society that cannot create wealth and the well-being of its citizens. So for reasons that are not ideological but have to do with human suffering, these countries have come to understand that state resources emerge from the nation and not by providence, that every cent that the former spends is paid by the society as a whole. A growing lucidity in this matter has brought the topic of the state to the political arena. We have come to ask ourselves seriously, what are the real functions of the state?

If they are to be carried out efficiently, such functions should be very few. There are, first of all, the necessary functions of security and defense. Although in light of recent developments in Peru one cannot help feeling a certain envy for the absence of an army in Costa Rica and the hope that Panama may follow suit in the near future. The narco-guerrillas and terrorist groups in Latin America have forced our armies to assume roles in the defense of the nation. In the case of Peru, we have seen the extent to which this is dangerous for democracy. At the same time it is utopian to think that we can completely do away with these armed forces in the struggle against tens of thousands of subversives. But what we must recognize is that giving forces of law and order administrative responsibility in certain zones (as was done in Peru) guarantees political instability and harms general freedom, and it does not secure success against the enemy.

The state is also responsible for organizing the population in cases of emergencies like earthquakes or hurricanes. There are also certain services where it may not be easy or fair to charge: the registry of property and statistics. In our case, however, such administrative functions have always been a nest of corruption for various reasons: an overregulation, the absence of public watchfulness regarding the creation of norms, and a lack of information among average citizens. There has also been the discretionary power of the functionary who becomes a source of authority rather than service, and the absence of really independent juridical processes to dissuade an abusive or corruptible official. There has been centralism forcing the concentration of a large number of cases. There is a bureaucracy aimed at justifying the work of useless functionaries with even more rule making. In this aspect we need a serious review of our norms with an eye to simplification within a clear process that informs citizens of all requirements. The reduction of the participation of the state and its bureaucracy, as well as a state decentralization, is a sine qua non for a worthwhile deregulation.

The government must also struggle against the monopolies, which are a sort of fifth column conspiring within the market, but only to the extent to which they limit private activity and not if they are the result of free market interplay. The great monopolist in Peru today is the state. Anticapitalist propaganda tirelessly accuses the large private consortiums (the large private consortiums in Peru are considerably weaker than in many other parts of Latin America) of practicing monopolization. They forget that state monopoly in a multitude of areas is the major obstacle for free competition. Privatization, so long as it does not transfer a protected monopoly to a private firm, is one of the best ways a country like Peru has of bringing in the kind of justice called for by the socialists. It implies taking economic fiefdom away from the richest of all, the government. And the critics of capitalism forget when they lash out against monopolies that institutions they supposedly favor, like trade unions, are part of the problem. They function as monopolies, too. It is a shame that the only really serious reform in the Latin American trade union movement was carried out under the infamous Pinochet dictatorship in Chile. Rather than speak well of the dictatorship, this speaks very poorly of Latin American democracy.

In Peru the trade unions and labor legislation born under the coercion of labor pressure groups have become in recent years a great obstacle to the creation of legal employment, because the businessman has come to look upon the worker as a burden. Unionized workers in Peru amount to scarcely 11 percent of the employed population. Those suffering from the situation make up the immense majority of the working population. And of course jobs generated by the "informal" economy are at a disadvantage, because there is no legal protection against any abuses. This is a typical case where the Peruvian state should step aside since its interference impedes job creation and forces many to live in the parallel economy; instead it should expand its presence as a guarantor of the legal rights of those workers currently involved in the "underground" economy. The state protecting the worker has ended up leaving the vast majority of Peruvian workers unprotected.

It is not fair for the government to turn the sick, the elderly, or the handicapped over to competition. The obligation, therefore, of insurance does not seem excessive. This does not mean that the person without a penny to pay for insurance dies or goes to prison. A state, which is the entity that collects taxes, can establish a system of negative taxes to benefit that percentage of the citizens without resources not only to pay taxes, but even to cover their basic necessities. With a compulsory minimun insurance covering retirement, illness, handicaps, and unemployment, the state meets its social responsibility. By pulling apart the inefficient and corrupt social security system currently in effect in Peru and making it private, the state could make sure this responsibility is met, as opposed to something inspired by social justice but which is simply unjust in practice. Besides, it would eliminate the obligation of holding back a percentage of the employee's salary only to end up in government pockets. Citizens in a free society should be able to administer their incomes as they please, giving health and retirement the importance they wish. In a society like that of Peru there will always be a sector unable to pay for such insurance. In this case a negative tax becomes a sort of state subsidy, but only a limited one, offered precisely to people who need it and administered smoothly. In such a case the state does not disappear: it becomes the arbiter in an efficient and fair system. In a country like Peru where the economic system is divided into a legal zone, a gray area, and a massive illegal zone, the privatization of social services within the bounds of competition would, in effect, go a long way toward integrating the legal and illegal economies.

Putting education in private hands is another great Latin American taboo. Education was one of the major points of conflict in the Peruvian electoral campaign of 1990. Once again, reality here has transformed the illusions of those defending the educative role of the state into a farce. State education in Peru is a disaster. In practice parents have ended up paying for it due to subtle and insidious administrative practices. In many places the students and families themselves have had to contribute to the construction of schoolrooms with bricks, cement, and other materials. Making education private does not mean eliminating state education. It means establishing healthy competition among all and offering families the option to select. Following the principle of negative taxes, the state should finance, via loans to be paid by the student once he or she has become part of the work force, the sort of education in question. A person choosing a more expensive center of learning should pay for it.

The role of the state as a collector of taxes should be seriously revised in Latin America. The redistributive state has been one of our great tragedies. Such a state has forgotten, or never knew, that the best distributor of wealth is the market. This notion of fiscal redistribution, which all the so-called liberal governments are once again calling for today in Latin America, has meant that individual states devour a great part of the wealth created by citizens without any services rendered to compensate for the loss. By doing this, they have raised the costs for individuals and firms and therefore harmed the very creation of wealth.

In Peru there is a tangle of taxes, several of which are not even spelled out, that has had a triple effect: a rise in tax evasion, more people moving into the underground economy, and the discouragement of foreign and domestic investment. The Fujimori government has perpetuated the tendency of its predecessors to depend, for the survival of the treasury, on gasoline taxes. It has also continued the tradition of generating instability by decreeing, and then doing away with, new taxes week by week within a confused fiscal system that is sending out bad signals to private enterprise. The poor handling of the general sales taxes (IGV), for example, has made for ongoing protests on the part of both wholesalers and retailers. Not only its erratic nature has had negative effects, but also its intake, which amounts to 18 percent since mid-1992. The Peruvian state could collect taxes in a far more efficient and just manner if it did away with the current tax labyrinth and chose to collect only personal income taxes. Once again, in the case of income tax, the negative tax system could be at the service of the poor.

But perhaps the most important role the state must play in any society, and it is done poorly in Latin America, is the administration of justice. If one had to choose one among all state institutions contributing in recent times to Peruvian and Latin American underdevelopment, the justice system would doubtless win. When the enemies of liberalism accuse liberalism of wanting to do away with the state, they do not recognize that its vision of society depends on the state the way lungs depend on oxygen, and that without the state no society can be called civil. This was very well explained by the English philosopher Thomas Hobbes when he offered, three centuries ago, his famous description of man as the wolf of man. In an underdeveloped society like ours a state with the power to make regulations work and dissuade or punish violators is indispensable, since the essential definition of an underdeveloped society has cultural rather than economic connotations. Our culture is one of debasement of the law: it is not complied with, it is bought, it is changed overnight, and it is imposed on some while others are exempt. We have seen that the sense of justice brought in by Mr. Fujimori in Peru suffers from the same defects of all its predecessors. It is the emanation of political power. It is impregnated with juridical positivism. It operates on the premise that legality is an instrument that we apply in an unequal manner depending upon the subject in question, and is corrupt from top to bottom. It regards justice as an instrument of government, as a policy in itself, rather than as an abstract notion wider than particular governments ruling the conduct of society over time. Such notions as private enterprise and market economy are unthinkable in a free society without an effective, decent, and powerful justice system. This does not exclude private arbitration, one of the great wisdoms in a civilized society. Private arbitration is already practiced in a rather elementary form in an important sector of Peruvian society, despite the law, since, once again, such practice is rooted only in the underground economy. But so long as there is an absence of institutions that represent the whole of society and while existing ones do not allow for the reconciliation of the legal economy and the underground economy within the same law, Peru's administration of justice will remain a dead letter.

Since property is not robbery, as nineteenth-century French philosopher Pierre Proudhon claimed, but the very substance of freedom, a state protecting the rights to property is a state at the service of its citizens. In a country such as Peru, then, creating a society made of citizens is as urgent as promoting justice for all. It must be a society of property holders where it makes sense for justice to defend the right to property. It must be a society of business people where it makes sense for justice to defend the rights of business. It must be a society of free men and women where it makes sense for justice to defend freedom. In our case the absence of authentic justice has been one of the greatest causes of underdevelopment in every sense of the word, cultural as well as economic. And the absence of democracy, which has marked our republican history throughout the present and past centuries, has been one of the major causes of the absence of authentic justice. The government of Alberto Fujimori has recently become part of this odious tradition.

Liberalism has frequently been accused of promoting inequality. This seems especially cruel in poverty-ridden Latin America. In fact, inequality is a precious thing. In the words of the famous nineteenth-century

Spanish writer, Leopoldo Alas Clarín, "Democracy should mean an equality of conditions, an equality of *means* for all, so that the inequality which is later determined by life emerges from differences in faculties, not from social artifice. In any case society should be egalitarian, but with respect for the work of Nature, which is not."

In Latin America the egalitarian efforts of government after government have produced the worst forms of inequality and discrimination that any state policy could imagine. In the particular case of Peru we have seen how the state and its governments have forced literally millions of citizens into illegality and how political power itself has become a major source of enrichment, because functionaries made money from it or because specific private groups in collusion with it took legal advantage. This has happened with governments, leaning right or leaning left, which were espousing equality.

There is nothing better to be offered a human being than the diversity that seems to be part and parcel of human nature. This is why liberalism is the natural ally of the human condition, as opposed to that egalitarian artifice that socialism and populism have wanted to set up (with no success and creating worse forms of inequality) among us. Uruguayan writer José Enrique Rodó, the author of *Ariel*, a book that is as widely misunderstood as it is read, rightly claimed that the duty of the state is to facilitate the use of one's own means in order to stimulate in a uniform fashion the uncovering of human superiority wherever it might exist. In this way and above and beyond this kind of social equality, "all inequality is justified because it is sanctioned by the mysterious selections of Nature or the deserving efforts of one's will."

Of course this equality of rights and opportunities does not literally mean an equality of conditions. It indicates the real possibility of achieving things that only one's own efforts can guarantee. Along these lines, privatization in Peru, as long as it spreads property ownership on a massive scale, can be a state instrument for the creation of a certain equality of opportunity. There is a kind of moral obligation in this as well: the state is largely responsible for the lack of a large number of owners and of an extensive and solid middle class.

This is why there must also be an institutional reform allowing that vast sector known as the underground economy to become legal. In this way their rich social contribution, which is responsible today for a wide percentage of economic activity in Peru, could shake off the shackles confining it. Thus, they would contribute to the country's prosperity, not just, as is the case now, to its subsistence. Neither in Peru nor in any other Latin American country has there been a massive reform incorporating this parallel society to the ease and security of the legal institutional framework. What is more, we find many forces working against this. In 1992, for example, the Fujimori government uprooted by force in several sectors of metropolitan Lima and even the center of the capital thousands of street vendors who were earning their livings on the pavements of Lima and had become veritable symbols of the shadow economy. This policy was only a continuation of the old error of considering the Peruvian involved in the informal economy as an enemy or a delinquent.

Emerson said that nations should be judged according to a minority and not a majority of its people. I am afraid that in Latin America such a formula would mean condemnation. We are a world of majorities stripped by small, and at times very small, minorities of the possibilities of well-being. And in this sad story of the Latin American state mercantilism has played (directly and indirectly) an unfortunate and evil role. We Latin Americans did not invent this system. It was already in effect in the Europe that emerged four or five centuries ago from the shadows of the Middle Ages, tearing away, with the appearance of a market economy, the social organization prevailing until then. But we have perfected this system to a mad extreme. No liberal reform is possible as long as we do not endow the state with a value that is both ethical and practical, essential when establishing a market economy: that of neutrality. The famous *sandinista piñata* (the division of public goods among party members and leaders in Nicaragua just before handing power over to Mrs. Violeta Chamorro in 1990) is only one extreme symptom of a generalized evil on the continent; it blatantly and harmfully affects the relationships between authority and property, authority and enterprise, and the few and the many in any given nation. When the road to success becomes the market and not the hallway of a ministry or delinquency, we will see real liberalism instead of that liberal caricature, which, owing to a great contemporary confusion, has been attributed to our present Latin American nations.

How could we call corrupt governments like that of Collor de Mello in Brazil liberal? Corruption violates a fundamental principle, it is a degenerate form of redistribution and, of course, an enemy of what upholds freedom: the law. How could anyone have called Mr. Fujimori a liberal when he has governed since April 1992 in the company of some of the most corrupt military men in Latin America in collusion with drug dealers of Alto Huallaga? How can we be thinking of liberalism when we consider the rotten system in Venezuela where there is an ineptitude tempered only by a corruption that is a source of wealth for a large number of people? How can anyone say that Paraguay has become a liberal paradise when we see there an endemic corruption (revealed toward the end of 1992) among the highest military officers?

A great Peruvian, the Inca Garcilaso de la Vega, called his country a "step-mother of its children." The same might be said of the Latin American state. As in the case of all stepmothers, this one inspires fear and sometimes terror, which explains why a good portion of Latin American governments have dared to liberalize prices and lower tariffs but have not seen fit to undertake the most difficult and essential of all liberal reforms for Latin American society: that of the state itself. Conspiring against this we see powerful interests and an overwhelming legacy. Today more than ever there is the opportunism of those last-moment converts who have suddenly been forced to turn away from populism because there is no way to pay for it but who cannot or will not accompany the measures of stabilization and liberalization with a reform, which would give their policies real sense. The specter of failure, then, is more real than ever. The tragic case of Peru should serve as a warning for the rest of the continent. One of the main tasks that lie ahead for the cause of freedom is to fight day and night against confusion. Goethe said that the only man worthy of life and liberty is he who is willing to conquer them for himself day after day. This is a timely reflection. The defenders of liberty have spent recent years explaining that which they were not, which they wanted to cast aside, which shocked them in contemporary life. Now it is time to explain what they are and what they want, because there are others who are beginning to usurp, sometimes unawares and sometimes with ill intentions, this very function.

Freedom has begun to win the battle of ideas around the world as a result of the living example of its virtues and the dying example of its enemies. In Latin America that battle has only just begun, surrounded by a remarkable absence of good examples. Thus, liberalism presents a formidable challenge.

Note

1. The *ejidos*, state-controlled land units in the Mexican countryside, were a symbol of the Mexican Revolution for years.

Bibliography

Americas Watch (AW). *Peru under Fire: Human Rights since the Return to Democracy.* Human Rights Watch Books. New Haven: Yale University Press, 1992.

Arce Borja, Luis, ed. *Guerra Popular en el Perú: el Pensamiento Gonzalo.* Brussels: Edición del Autor, June 1989.

Archer, Christon I. "The Army of New Spain and the Wars of Independence, 1790-1821." *Hispanic American Historical Review* 61:4 (November 1981).

Bakewell, Johnson and Dodge, eds. *Readings in Latin American History I. The Formative Centuries.* Durham: Duke University Press, 1985.

Basadre, Jorge. *Perú: Problema y Posibilidad.* 2d ed. Lima: Banco Internacional, 1978.

Chirinos Soto, Enrique. *La Nueva Constitución y los Partidos Políticos.* Lima: Centro Documentación Andina, 1984.

Clarín, Leopoldo Alas. "Estudio Crítico" published as a foreword to José Enrique Rodó's *Ariel.* Madrid: Espasa Calpe, 1948.

De Soto, Hernando. Letter addressed to Señor Fujimori, 28 January 1992.

De Soto, Hernando, and Enrique Ghersi. *El Otro Sendero.* Lima: El Barranco, 1986.

El Comercio. Lima: 10 November 1992.

Fukuyama, Francis. *The End of History and the Last Man.* New York: Free Press, 1992.

García Lupo, Rogelio. "Narcos Peruanos Delatan al Líder de *Sendero Luminoso.*" *Tiempo* (Madrid) (5 October 1992).

González, José. "Guerrillas and Coca in the Upper Huallaga Valley." In *Shining Path of Peru.* New York: St. Martin's Press, 1992.

Gorriti, Gustavo. *Sendero: Historia de la Guerra Milenaria del Perú,* vol.1. Lima: Apoyo, 1990.

Hayek, Friedrich A. *Law, Legislation and Liberty.* Chicago: University of Chicago Press, 1973-79.

Instituto de Desarrollo del Sector Informal. *Rostros de la Informalidad.* Lima: Instituto de Desarrollo del Sector Informal, 1992.

Instituto Libertad y Democracia. *El Comercio Ambulatorio de Lima*. Lima: Instituto Libertad y Democracia, 1989.

Iwasaki Cauti, Fernando. *Extremo Oriente y Perú en el Siglo XVI*. Madrid: MAPFRE, 1992.

Kaufman Purcell, Susan, and Blake Friscia. "A Growing Yen for Latin America." *Hemisfile* (New York) (May 1992).

Keith, Robert G. "Encomienda, Hacienda and Corregimiento in Spanish America: A Structural Analysis." *Hispanic American Historical Review* 51:3 (August 1971).

Matos Mar, José. *Desborde popular y Crisis del Estado: El Nuevo Rostro del Perú en la Década de 1980*. Lima: Instituto de Estudios Peruanos, 1984.

Morodo, Raúl. "Perú: Sendero Luminoso y Sendero Ominoso." *Debate Abierto* 8 (Revista de Ciencias Sociales)(Summer-Autumn 1992).

Revel, Jean-Francois. *Le Regain Démocratique*. Paris: Fayard, 1992.

Rodó, José Enrique. *Ariel*. Madrid: Espasa Calpe, 1948.(The first edition came out in 1900.)

Rowe, John H. "The Incas under Spanish Colonial Institutions." *Hispanic American Historical Review* 37:2 (May 1957).

Smith, Michael L. "Shining Path's Urban Strategy: Ate Vitarte." In *Shining Path of Peru*. New York: St. Martin's Press, 1992.

Stone Jeremy. *The Sendero File* 1,2,3,4.(July, August, September, October 1992)

Vargas Ugarte, Rubén. *Historia General del Perú*. Lima: Milla Batres, 1981.

Vargas Llosa, Mario. "Inquest in the Andes." *The New York Times Magazine*. (31 July 1983)

Index